CERVANTES'S *NOVELAS EJEMPLARES*

Purdue Studies in Romance Literatures

Editorial Board

Enrique Caracciolo-Trejo,
  Series Editor
Jeanette Beer
Paul B. Dixon

Floyd F. Merrell
Anthony Julian Tamburri
Allen G. Wood

Associate Editors

French
Jean Alter
Max Aprile
Paul Benhamou
Willard Bohn
Gerard J. Brault
Germaine Brée
Victor Brombert
Mary Ann Caws
Gérard Defaux
Ursula Franklin
Floyd F. Gray
Michael Issacharoff
Milorad R. Margitić
Glyn P. Norton
Allan H. Pasco
Gerald Prince
David Lee Rubin
English Showalter, Jr.

Italian
Fiora A. Bassanese
Peter Carravetta
Giuseppe C. Di Scipio
Benjamin Lawton

Luso-Brazilian
Fred M. Clark
Joaquim-Francisco Coelho

Mary L. Daniel
Marta Peixoto

Spanish and Spanish American
Lida Aronne-Amestoy
J. B. Avalle-Arce
Frank P. Casa
Ivy A. Corfis
James O. Crosby
Frederick A. de Armas
Edward Friedman
David T. Gies
Roberto González Echevarría
Patricia Hart
David K. Herzberger
Djelal Kadir
Lucille Kerr
Marvin A. Lewis
Howard Mancing
Alberto Moreiras
Randolph D. Pope
Geoffrey Ribbans
Francisco Ruiz Ramón
Elżbieta Skłodowska
Josep Miquel Sobrer
Catherine Swietlicki
Mario Valdés
Howard Young

 volume 10

CERVANTES'S *NOVELAS EJEMPLARES*

Between History and Creativity

Joseph V. Ricapito

Purdue University Press
West Lafayette, Indiana

Copyright © 1996 by Purdue Research Foundation. All rights reserved.

04   03   02   01   00   5   4   3   2   1

First paperbound printing, November 1999

Printed on acid-free paper in the United States of America
Design by Anita Noble

Library of Congress Cataloging-in-Publication Data
Ricapito, Joseph V.
    Cervantes's Novelas ejemplares : between history and creativity / Joseph V. Ricapito.
      p.   cm. — (Purdue studies in Romance literatures ; v. 10)
    Includes bibliographical references and index.
    ISBN 1-55753-078-5 (alk. paper)
    1. Cervantes Saavedra, Miguel de, 1547–1616. Novelas ejemplares. 2. Literature and society—Spain. 3. Social problems in literature. 4. Spain—In literature. I. Title. II. Series.
PQ6324.Z5R53 1996
863'.3—dc20   95-49291
                                                                                 CIP

ISBN 1-55753-204-4 (pbk. : alk. paper)

This book is dedicated to the memory of

Dr. Paul J. Salvatore,
Professor of Romance Languages
and past chair of that department of
Brooklyn College
of
The City University of New York.

His generous concern, wise guidance, and counsel
made my career and that of many others possible.

Contents

ix Acknowledgments
1 Introduction
11 Chapter One
  "La gitanilla":
  At the Crossroads of History and Creativity
39 Chapter Two
  Católicos secretos, Conversos,
    and the Myth of the Maritime Life
    in "La española inglesa"
69 Chapter Three
  "El licenciado Vidriera,"
    or "La historia de un fracaso"
97 Chapter Four
  The Prose of Honor
121 Chapter Five
  Apologia pro patria sua:
    Cervantes's "La señora Cornelia"
135 Notes
151 Selected Bibliography
159 Index

Acknowledgments

I have read briefer versions of these chapters at scholarly meetings, and the many suggestions and critical comments offered to me have found their way into this book. I owe a debt of gratitude to the staff of the Interlibrary Loan section of the Middleton Library of Louisiana State University and to Louisiana State University for a sabbatical leave during which time I pursued research on this book.

I wish to thank my wife, Carolyn, my critic and editor, who worked generously to see to it that my writing reflected exactly what I was thinking. I also express to her my thanks for her wonderful support during this and other times.

My thanks go also to Samuel G. Armistead, who has always offered his moral support and his extensive knowledge, and to whom I am forever grateful; to John Johnson (Authors' Agent) Limited for permission to quote from Alison Plowden's *Danger to Elizabeth;* and to Amanda Schlatre, Karen Powell, and Aaron Simon, whose computer skills assisted in the preparation of the final manuscript.

Introduction

Some years ago in a conversation after a lengthy and enjoyable dinner at La Carmencita in Madrid, Stephen Gilman summed up a part of our conversation by saying that one believed either that literature was a product of creative imagination, or that it was inspired by life. Knowing his work as I do, there was no question that his answer favored the latter. For myself I must say that there is no vacillation either. I fully embrace the notion that literary production is largely from life and experience (my best models being Fernando de Rojas and Miguel de Cervantes), where the "circumstance," as Ortega y Gasset would say, molds and structures our thoughts and works.

It is with this premise that I have written the following chapters. My title reflects this history/creativity (i.e., literature) dichotomy. It does not imply or intend a "crunch" between the two. I am using the term *history* to signify the author's time (the time period in which the author lives), and *creativity* to mean the verbal, literary, communicative mode. I have explored this dichotomy in some of the *novelas* of Cervantes that illustrate the human dimensions and existential correlations to historical experience.

Although I am interested in the historical part of the history/literature equation, considerable artistic creation and manipulation goes into any literary work. The artistic considerations occur at a stage after the writer's initial involvement in the writing task. One can agree with Benedetto Croce that there is a crucial moment in a writer's psychological and intellectual makeup that we can call, for lack of a more precise term, inspiration.

To be sure, alongside Cervantes, the social and political critic, there was Cervantes, the humanist, the literary critic, and the

Introduction

polemicist. It would be an incredible task to pinpoint with any degree of accuracy when and how the process of response, selection, and literary activity took place. Suffice it to say that one of the stages of postinspiration deals with literary tradition. The creation had to belong to a body or genre that Cervantes thought important and worthy. In my view, the only truly worthy vessel into which Cervantes poured his *creatio* was the one that had achieved prominence in all of Europe—Boccaccio and the Italian frame novel tradition. Even where the Spanish tradition was autochthonous, Boccaccio and the Italianate tradition were at the literary forefront and created an ideal of literature with which Cervantes obviously wished to be identified. The public expected such an association for a writer who hoped to achieve recognition beyond the borders of his country. Cervantes chose to associate himself with the tradition that had achieved success in Spain either through the Italian originals or through translations printed by Valencian publishers. Attachment to the Italianate tradition represents the second part of the division between history and art, but it is a secondary stage of *praxis* rather than the initial conception of the urge to create with words. There are other features to the external incentives that serve as the creative impulse in the works.

The statement of Ginés de Pasamonte (*Don Quijote* 1.22) has assumed an almost independent existence and has become an index of Cervantes's awareness of literary vogues and styles. When he speaks of his *Vida,* he associates it with *Lazarillo de Tormes* and other similar works. In this enunciation by the wily Ginés, the absences and silences are just as important as the words spoken.

In approaching the study of *Las novelas ejemplares,* I see two important keys that may easily have determined the path that Cervantes chose. Perhaps one of the most important prose writers of Cervantes's time was Mateo Alemán. His *Guzmán de Alfarache* achieved great popularity, and his work became a model. The *Guzmán,* with its interpolated stories carefully composed to complement the moral-didactic purposes of the work, stood as a monument of literary accomplishment. But Alemán's masterpiece offered a one-sided view of human experience.[1] His stories treated love, but love was subordinated to other concerns. The resulting product failed to include other, more regenerating features of love and experience. This was a challenge for Cervantes.

To return to Ginés's silences, one involved the *Guzmán* and Alemán, and this reticence is perhaps understandable. *Guzmán de Alfarache* was a very significant work. It contained many of the features that Cervantes believed should go into a narrative—an identifiable time and space, characters involved in moral questions that reflected attitudes of the time, a concern with fiction as a problem of referentiality. But the central vision of the work with its pessimism simply was not a part of Cervantes's view of human experience. *Las novelas ejemplares* is one vehicle for Cervantes to rectify this somber view in a brief fashion; he does so in a fuller manner with *Don Quijote*.[2]

It is my belief and one of the theses of this book that it is against the background of Lope de Vega and Mateo Alemán that the reader must read and judge the *novelas* of Cervantes. His career as dramatist has been dealt with by others; I do not intend to study his dramatic works. What we know of his career as a man of the theater is that it was largely one of imitation and it was generally unsuccessful. Cervantes and just about every other person working in the genre were overshadowed by the towering figure and work of Lope de Vega. The relations between Cervantes and Lope were not the best, to judge from some comments made by Lope. Cervantes's theater never achieved the free, exuberant spontaneity of Lope's plays, although the honor theme so often treated by Lope was equally of interest to Cervantes. Several of the *novelas* treat this theme, but Cervantes circumvents the rivalry by tacitly acknowledging Lope's superiority in the dramatic form, though not in the area of short fiction (something that Lope attempted to resolve after the publication of *Las novelas ejemplares* with short stories of his own). A certain amount of Cervantes's writing (both the shorter and longer narratives) is aimed at competing with the tremendous appeal of *Guzmán de Alfarache* as a narrative and the monopolization of the honor theme by Lope.

The foregoing are literary and social incentives to creation. When we refer to the history in and behind the stories, we are acknowledging that Cervantes was acutely aware of the problems of his time, that the stories are not the product of a simple literary situation, and that the works are a result of this awareness.

Introduction

To be precise, history is not a by-product, it is the warp and woof of the *novelas* themselves. It is not a separate isolatable quantity that could be excised from the work, leaving behind its *creatio*. Cervantes has placed his characters and their problems *into* history, and what has emerged is a *historia novelada.* The *novelas* are a glimpse of Cervantes's Spain and include a cataloguing of the social, political, and historical problems of the time. Cervantes presents historical events and applies a critique to them through his characters and their human situations.

It is through this lens that I believe one must approach the reading of *Las novelas ejemplares:* a literary creation whose substance is historical in nature and consists of the history that Cervantes lived. The various messages (not in a didactic-moral sense) that come through concern problems related to Spain's minorities (*conversos* and Gypsies); social mobility in a Christian setting; the presence in society of differing and even outlandish individuals; the waning power and prestige of Spain in the world; the oppressive role of *honra* in society; and an awareness of literary genres, e.g., Cervantes's insistence on the differences between the picaresque genre, symbolized by Alemán's *Guzmán de Alfarache,* and Cervantes's own gentler vision of human behavior.[3]

The picture of Cervantes that should emerge from the chapters that follow is not that of a humanist who only focused on literature and literary problems, but that of a Spaniard concerned with the historical and social events of his time. His view was stern; his critique, sharp. Cervantes was characterized by a sensitivity that responded to external stimuli around him. He was a critic of his time and place in every sense.

At the same time one should never forget that Cervantes functioned as a "professional writer," and like all professional writers he had a public to acknowledge. In the course of his work there were compromises to be made, as I show in my analysis of "La gitanilla," a story that presents a covert sense of disagreement with current laws and mores regarding Gypsies and *conversos.* At the moment of writing, Cervantes knew that his public was keen on tales that abounded in the supernatural, like the chivalric romance, or the desperate love stories of the sentimental romance, or the adventures of the picaresque romance. His writing was suffused with the felicitous improbabilities of the Greek romance. These were the reigning literary pleasures of his public. Alemán serves as a good example of a writer whose work was successful in a commercial way. In no wise different, Cervantes faced his public, but at the same time he wrote "between the lines" in a way that enabled him to vent his various angers and frustrations, his resentments and disappointments like the less-than-exuberant welcome he received on his return from his imprisonment in Algiers, his various jailings in Spain, or other defeats of a personal nature. His work is often an inner settlement between the public gusto and his own more personal strivings. This is to be seen in "La gitanilla" and "La señora Cornelia" or in the quest for freedom in "Rinconete y Cortadillo" and "La ilustre fregona." Cervantes's work must be measured in terms of public clamor and the individual, indeed, private and personal aspirations and strivings. The resultant literary products contain this conflict, and it is to be found in so many of his best works. This personal, existential situation of Cervantes, in my opinion, bleeds through the text so that next to the idealistic, fantastic, wonderfully improbable episodes, we have scenes of death, disorder, murder, madness, illness, or other forms of mayhem. There lies at the heart of *Las novelas ejemplares* a tension between public expectation and the thrust of integrity and originality. The final product is, as I have hoped to show, a blend between intertextuality, history, literary creation, and, for want of a better but nevertheless still very useful term, the *personalismo* of Cervantes. My use of the term *public* is similar to that made by Kristen G. Brookes or John Weiger as well as James Parr.[4] They refer to a "reader" in the text and outside the text. My use regards a body of literate population with a developed sense of literary vogues and currents, and it is to this group that Cervantes felt a sense of responsibility.

It is a tribute to the importance of *Las novelas ejemplares* that some of the most influential Hispanists have studied them. Ramón Menéndez Pidal, Francisco Rodríguez Marín, Américo Castro, Joaquín Casalduero, Agustín González de Amezúa, Marcel Bataillon, among older critics; followed by Juan Bautista Avalle-Arce, Peter Dunn, Manuel Durán, Francisco Márquez Villanueva, Ruth El Saffar, Albert A. Sicroff, Julio Rodríguez

Introduction

Luis, Harry Sieber, Elias Rivers, Carroll B. Johnson, Maurice Molho, Agustín Redondo, Thomas Hart, and Alban K. Forcione, and, most recently, Steven Hutchinson. It is a tremendous challenge to write on a work that has received the attention of such important intellects. The approach I have taken is surely not new, but one that claims a new awareness. Works like Johnson's enlightening article on "La española inglesa" merely show the need and the place for a "readjustment" to a *lectura histórica* of these *novelas* such as I have done. The critics mentioned brought to the *novelas* their own critical apparatus and the methodology current during their own time. This is true as much for Menéndez Pidal as it is for Hutchinson, whose approach assimilates the more recent (i.e., poststructuralist) methodologies of literary criticism. A study of *Las novelas ejemplares* and its critical practitioners is indeed a survey of the history of literary criticism.

All of the above-mentioned scholars brought fresh insights to an understanding of the *novelas,* but I wish to focus on two of them and one other critic. Américo Castro, Alban K. Forcione, and Stephen Greenblatt are important to this study because their ideas and methodologies touch upon what I have attempted.

Don Américo's landmark research opened the way for bold perspectives on Cervantes particularly and Spanish Golden Age literature generally. There are admittedly differences in his points of view between *El pensamiento de Cervantes* and later works, but essentially I have accepted his view of what can be called the "two Cervantes," the existence of a public persona and a private one. A reading of *Las novelas ejemplares* shows, in my view, the author as a vacillating character; there is to be seen a subtle play on levels of meaning and interpretation that says one thing in the prologue, yet in the body of the *novelas* does other things. It reveals a surface conformity with the literary canons of declared exemplarity.

There is also in the course of the *novelas* a desire for conformity to current mores and practices: "La gitanilla," "La ilustre fregona," "Rinconete y Cortadillo," "La fuerza de la sangre," "Las dos doncellas," and others. Cervantes's twisting of the inner dynamics of his tales avoids "radical" solutions that would challenge the mores by which Spaniards lived, himself included. Castro notes some resistance by Cervantes to some of the questionable mores of his time, and this is woven subtly into the fabric of the *novelas,* as I hope to show in several instances. There is every reason to accept the idea of the "two Cervantes."

Castro's views of the presence and meaning of *conversos* and other minority groups in Spain also find a welcome home in my own ideas and probably constitute the *maestro*'s greatest contribution to the literary and social history of Spain's Golden Age, just as they did in the works of Gilman, Joseph H. Silverman, Samuel G. Armistead, Márquez Villanueva, and others.

Forcione's two important books call for a different consideration. He has contributed decisively to Cervantes studies and has illuminated numerous works of Cervantes. However, I accept Castro's view of the "two Cervantes" and reject Forcione's view of the Erasmianism of *Las novelas ejemplares.* Although he sustains his theory with much erudition, it strikes me that the Erasmian influence Forcione discusses appears in Spain much earlier than the seventeenth century. By the time of the composition of the *novelas* (as elusive as their chronology is) a different religious spirit had taken over, as Castro and Gilman show. The Counter-Reformation had a stronger, more severe view of human experience and religious strivings, as the works of Alemán, Tirso de Molina, and Pedro Calderón de la Barca illustrate. Cervantes belongs more to this latter period (although on spiritual questions admittedly his position does not appear to be as severe as those of Alemán, Tirso, and Calderón) than to that of the Erasmianism of *Lazarillo de Tormes,* Alfonso de Valdés, and others. Cervantes's is a different spiritual atmosphere from the sixteenth century, when Erasmus's writings and thought flourished in Spain. While we have all profited from Casalduero's readings of Cervantine texts, their somewhat rigid adherence to a religious Counter-Reformation view, oftentimes at the expense of artistic features of the *novelas,* seems to ignore the more social and existential effects on characters and actions found in the *novelas. Las novelas ejemplares* seems to follow another path: a combination of history and creativity, which I have brought into the title of this book. Cervantes is creating an "historical exemplarity" or "exemplary histories" much in the same manner that Elsa Morante would write a book called *La storia: un romanzo,* or similar to what John Dos Passos

Introduction

creates with his *USA Trilogy*. I read in the *novelas* a strong historical presence and concern that goes beyond Renaissance preoccupations with mimesis and verisimilitude.

In 1980, Greenblatt published an important book in the field of Renaissance studies: *Renaissance Self-Fashioning*. In this work, he laid out the design for a new critical historic modality, currently referred to as "New Historicism." He notes that in the sixteenth century there was new stress on the power of self-will on the individual as well as on objects of scholarly and literary contemplation (1). There was, he states, an increased self-consciousness about "the fashioning of human identity as a manipulable, artful process" (2), the term *fashioning* being identified with the development of the self. This development refers to the direction of the individual to the world, as well as a consistent mode of perceiving and behaving. If taken separately, Greenblatt states,

> it [self-fashioning] suggests representation of one's nature or intention in speech or actions. And with representation we return to literature, or rather we may grasp that self-fashioning derived its interest precisely from the fact that it functions without regard for a sharp distinction between literature and social life. It invariably crosses the boundaries between the creation of literary characters, the shaping of one's own identity, the experience of being molded by forces outside one's control, the attempt to fashion other selves. Such boundaries may, to be sure, be strictly observed in criticism, just as we may distinguish between literary and behavioral styles, but in doing so we pay a high price, for we begin to lose a sense of the complex interactions of meaning in a given culture. We wall off literary symbolism from the symbolic structures operative elsewhere, as if art alone were a human creation, as if humans themselves were not, in Clifford Geertz's phrase, cultural artifacts. (3)

Thus the literature produced in this time includes the particular behavior of an author, "the expression of the codes by which behavior is shaped, and as a reflection upon these codes ..." (4). Consequently, any viewing of literature in this manner takes from it "a system of signs that constitutes a given culture; its proper goal, however difficult to realize, is a *poetics of culture* [Greenblatt's emphasis]" (5). For Greenblatt,

Introduction

> Social actions are themselves always imbedded in systems of public signification, always grasped, even by their makers, in acts of interpretation, while the words that constitute the works of literature ... are by their very nature the manifest assurance of a similar embeddedness. Language, like other sign systems, is a collective construction; our interpretative task must be to grasp more sensitively the consequences of this fact by investigating both the social presence to the world of the literary text and the social presence of the world in the literary text. (5)

Greenblatt does not see the social panorama and the literary product as separate systems but rather as binomial ones that at one point intersect to form single, binary composed signs.

> their significance for us is not that we see *through* [Greenblatt's emphasis] them [resonant texts] to underlying and prior historical principles but rather that we may interpret the interplay of their symbolic structures with those perceivable in the careers of their authors and in the larger social world as constituting a single, complex process of self-fashioning and, through this interpretation, come closer to understanding how literary and social identities were formed in this culture. (5–6)

He suggests ten conditions as part of his interpretation, and of these, two are of particular importance to Cervantes's work in *Las novelas ejemplares*: "2. Self-fashioning for such figures involves submission to an absolute power or authority situated at least partially outside the self—God, a sacred book, an institution such as church, court" and "3. Self-fashioning is achieved in relation to something perceived as alien, strange, or hostile" (9). Both of these keys can be perceived in the *novelas* of Cervantes.

It would take another book to refute Forcione's Erasmian interpretation of the *novelas*, and since this concern does not fall within the scope I have laid out for this work, I see no need to practice what I think can be called "negative criticism." I can only admire his fruitful and erudite insights and conclude that we merely disagree. It is for this reason that the subject of the Erasmianism of the works does not occupy a place in my own work and I do not take up this important question in my analyses.

Introduction

Readers may find critical works that refer to the individual *novelas* absent from my approach. I did not intend to provide a critical history of each story; I focused on those works that fell within my historical concern. Criticism of Cervantes's works is produced in on-going waves, and it is not always useful to be all-inclusive for the mere purpose of doing so.

For similar reasons, not all of the *novelas* are submitted to an historical analysis. I do not deem it necessary that every one be so treated. Instead, I have examined the subject of history in literature in a precise way in those stories that are strongly representative of this concern.

Chapter One

"La gitanilla"

At the Crossroads of History and Creativity

I

It has been the destiny of "La gitanilla" to be regarded benignly as a tale dealing with love, involving a Gypsy girl and a non-Gypsy youth, and this perception has tended to give the story a kind of saccharine taste. The love component dominated in the eyes of readers and, indeed, many critics. However, after studying carefully the history of Gypsies in Spain, I believe that this story deals with issues that go beyond young love.

Gypsies began to arrive in the Spanish peninsula in approximately 1425. At that time relations between Gypsies and the resident Spanish were good, and the Gypsies were looked upon as "pilgrims." They became numerous in the fifteenth century and moved about in large groups. Although at first they had been considered harmless, in the late fifteenth century they came to be regarded as dangerous "vagabonds." By 1499, the Catholic Kings had proclaimed 2,000 edicts against them.

What the sixteenth-century monarchies did to Jews and Moors was also done to Gypsies. They became victims of the same biases and life-threatening prejudices. In the Cortes of 1595 Gypsies were associated with Moors and Jews, and by 1610 they were compared unfavorably with Moors. The Pragmatic of 1499 was extended and modified several times throughout the sixteenth century. Bernard Leblon, a perceptive commentator of Gypsies in the Golden Age context, remarks:

> Il faut remarquer, à ce sujet, que les Gitans de Cervantes sont en perpétuelle infraction. En 1610, ils sont toujours assujettis à la pragmatique des Rois Catholiques de 1499, renouvelée et modifiée à la demande des Cortes, par Charles V, en 1525, 1528, 1534, et 1539, et par Philippe II en 1560 et

Chapter One

en 1586. Tous les Gitans sans domicile fixe et sans profession sont passibles de 6 ans de galères et les femmes, Gitanes ou non, qui se promèneraient en costume de Gitane sont condamnées à 100 coups de fouet et au banissement.[1]

It should be especially noted for its relevance to "La gitanilla" that Philip II came out decidedly against Gypsies and also those who dressed like them.[2] The *Novísima recopilación,* as shown by María Teresa Sánchez Ortega, records this progression of official sanction from the time of the Catholic Kings up to the reigns of Charles III and Charles IV (see Sánchez Ortega 25–26).

The pragmatic against those who live and dress like Gypsies was repeated by Philip IV. By 1745, as a result of pragmatics by Philip V, even the most fundamental rights accorded to all Spaniards were denied to Gypsies, e.g., the right of church refuge. Similar laws were passed in England, where in 1562 Queen Elizabeth denied Gypsies refuge in churches (Grande, "Los gitanos" 27c).

A new term was designated to refer to the Gypsies—"castellanos nuevos." The term obviously was modeled on the earlier "cristianos nuevos" that applied to converted Jews and Moors. "Castellanos nuevos" brought under its purview a people who were accused of numerous violations of social and spiritual life. In the eighteenth century the term became more than just an identifying marker; it became an insult.[3]

The bad animus against Gypsies was not confined to the Iberian peninsula; in France, King Louis XIV initiated a program against Gypsies, with punishment for Gypsy women and children.

Though a social minority, Gypsies were present in large numbers in Catalunia and Andalucia. Robert ter Horst speaks of the Gypsies as represented by small numbers and therefore relegates them to a marginality in society (89). Durán also notes their numbers as minimal (59) but cogently focuses on the literary artistry of Cervantes. Because Gypsies were a small segment of society, Durán suggests that Cervantes aimed his satire at other larger, perhaps more meaningful sectors of Spanish life. However, on the question of population size, Antonio Domínguez Ortiz speaks of Gypsy activities in a way that would involve greater numbers: "Los centenares o miles de gitanos ahorcados,

"La gitanilla"

linchados, enviados a presidio, a galeras, a la mina de Almadén, han permanecido en el anónimo" ("Documentación" 319). For him to speak of "centenares" and "miles" suggests Gypsies were a meaningful segment of the population.

Perhaps one of the most salient features of Gypsy life at the time was its homogeneity. It was a closed unit, but the act of closing in on itself was a defensive reaction to the hostility of non-Gypsy society. Gypsies had their own way of life, language, and customs, which were considered threatening to conventional Spanish life, and they defended their culture. They married according to their own rites, outside the jurisdiction of the church; they settled their own disputes. The long description of Gypsy life by the old Gypsy (see Cervantes 1: 100–03) is an attempt by Cervantes to present a sympathetic picture of the values by which Gypsies lived. The account has been described as idealistic, but it is so only inasmuch as it represents a great departure from the stereotypes that existed and are expressed in the work of Father Mariana and others. Forcione regards the Gypsy world in terms of "demonic" and "infernal" (passim) (just as the title of ter Horst's essay is taken from the Rimbaudian title ["A Season in Hell"]). Forcione makes a distinction between the King (with the attendant royal family/holy family) and humanity: "below the King we glimpse a demonic world opposing their redemptive efforts, and significantly it is presented in its aspect as a family" (95). Forcione furthermore emphasizes the "negative" aspects of the Gypsy world portrayed by the old Gypsy:

> On the other hand the Gypsy world, as a demonic order of lawlessness, terror, lust, and incest, forms the traditional lower world of romance in which an imprisoned heroine awaits the coming of a redeemer or a mysterious turn of providence that will restore her to her proper identity. (186)

Focusing on this world, he states,

> All of these elements—freedom, communism, pleasure, friendship, primitivism, simplicity, and natural vitality—are, of course, traditional themes of utopian and pastoral literature, and, since *La gitanilla* does initially expose the court society as a fallen, chaotic and sterile order, it is tempting

Chapter One

> to see the Gypsy community as a realm of essential values, a type of "green world," which exposes by contrast the deficiency of the real world and points toward the ideals that are to be impressed on reality if purification is to occur. (187–88)

While I can agree with Forcione's view of some of the "ideals" of the Gypsy life, I do not think that it is correct to speak of the Gypsy world as "demonic." This is precisely the kind of view that *gachó* society had. Obviously, Cervantes's presentation of Gypsies through certain "ideal" views would deny any assertion that he sees the Gypsy world as "infernal." Juan Manuel Montoya focuses on some cultural characteristics that differentiate between Gypsies and other groups:

> El mantenimiento de un amplio conjunto de tradiciones colectivas y pautas de comportamiento individual: rituales médicos, códigos de honor, ritos del ciclo vital (matrimoniales, funerarios, de nacimiento), resolución de los conflictos internos según los propios códigos, profundo respeto a los ancianos, etc. Tradiciones que se encuentran muy ligadas a una escala de valores basada más en la lógica simbólica que en la lógica racional, más propia ésta de los grupos occidentales mayoritarios. (30b, c)

But their particular lifestyle was removed from the flow of conventional life. In Leblon's words:

> Successivement créatures de Dieu et créatures du diable, les gitanes sont devenus à présent de dangereux anarchistes, qui menacent les fondements même de l'Etat. (*Gitans* 68)

Sancho de Moncada, one of the most powerful voices against Gypsies, presents what can be looked upon as a commonly held social view of them:

> gente ociosa, vagabunda y inútil a los Reinos, sin comercio, ocupación ni oficio alguno y si alguno tienen, es hacer ganzúas y garavatos para su profesión, siendo zánganos, que sólo viven de chupar y talar los reinos, sustentándose del sudor de los míseros labradores. (214–15)

In another passage Moncada inveighs against Gypsy women:

> Lo tercero, porque las gitanas son públicas rameras, comunes (a lo que se dice) a todos los gitanos, i con bailes, ademanes, palabras, i cantares torpes, hacen gran daño a las almas de los vasallos de V. Mag. siendo como es cosa notoria infinitos los daños que se han hecho en casas muy honestas. (Cited in Spanish by Leblon, *Gitans* 44–45)

Sánchez Ortega notes a genuine preoccupation of the government with the fact that the Gypsies possessed their own firearms:

> y también sus oficios, y modos de vivir, y todas las armas que tuvieren, así ofensivas, como defensivas, de cualquier género que sean, tanto las que tuvieren en las casas, como las que hubieren puesto en otras partes, o dado a guardar a otras personas, y los caballos, mulas, o otros animales que tuvieren para servirse de ellos, o para venderlos, o comerciarlos. (37)

While the focus of Sánchez Ortega's view is the eighteenth century in Spain, many of her observations are verified by other historians and observers of Spanish life, thereby making her views applicable to an earlier period. Criticism and stereotypes of Gypsies were fairly uniformly present from the fifteenth to the eighteenth centuries.

Reproducing part of a pragmatic that shows the degree to which the government obsessively and in a paranoiac manner oversaw the lives of Gypsies, Sánchez Ortega shows that no facet of their lives would be left unexamined:

> I. Que todos los que por partidas de Desposorios consta ser legítimamente casados in facie Ecclesia, y tener Ejecutorias, Provisiones del Consejo, u otras formales declaraciones de no ser Gitanos, o que en consecuencia de los vecindarios, que les estaban señalados, se verifique por información secreta, acompañada del informe de el Prelado, Párroco, o Párrocos respectivos, que vivían arreglados a las Reales Pragmáticas, Decretos y Ordenes del Consejo sean restituídos con sus mujeres, y hijos, que estaban bajo su patria potestad, y vivían en el mismo arreglo, a los propios Pueblos donde eran naturales, y tenían vecindad. (114)

The Gypsies' lifestyle together with their exotic looks created suspicion and fear on the part of society. Félix Grande quotes José Carlos Arévalo: "'En seguida se descubrió que los gitanos

Chapter One

eran los invitados falsos. Su exótico semblante, su connivencia [*sic*] con la magia, sus espejismos heréticos provocaron señales de alerta'" (*Memoria del flamenco* 93).

A curious phenomenon that became recorded in the pragmatics is the problem of people who joined Gypsy bands and lived among them, as Andrés did. The official reaction to such people was just as severe as the attitude toward genuine Gypsies:

> declaramos, que cualquier hombre, o mujer, que se aprendiere en el traje, y hábito de que hasta ahora ha usado este género de gente [Gypsies], o contra quien se probare haber usado de la lengua que ellos llaman jerigonza, sea tenido por Gitano para el efecto referido. (Sánchez Ortega 42)[4]

In a more positive way the government hoped to attract Gypsies away from Gypsy life toward a more "constructive" role in society. As Sánchez Ortega comments:

> Como ya hemos señalado, en ella se les permite toda la libertad en cuanto a oficios, lugar de residencia y forma de vida, siempre que abandonen su lengua y traje. Es decir, se les permite ser castellanos viejos, como a los demás, pero previamente han de haber renunciado a sus características propias. (157)

Assimilation, then, was the original aim of official Spanish policy.

But the Gypsies proved to be unwilling to abandon their way of life, their language, and their customs, and the government was not prepared to allow Gypsies merely to thrive on their own terms. The proscriptions were accompanied by more than threats. The threats were a means to control the Gypsies, but where possible the government aimed its efforts at extermination. Moncada asserts that after a period of time, any Gypsies who were still vagabonds should be put under the purview of "la ley del destierro perpetuo de España" (222). (These penalties [and others that I list throughout this chapter] were taken variously from several different sources: Clébert, Leblon, Sánchez Ortega, et al.)

Gypsies were deported in galley ships, exiled by decrees, brought together in ghettos, apprehended, and whipped. Some infractions were punished by cutting off the offender's ears (see Covarrubias: "En España los castigan [a los gitanos] severa-

"La gitanilla"

mente, y echan a los hombres a galeras, si no se arraygan y avezinan en alguna parte" [643a]). Others were jailed or put into slavery. The extermination process was not always physical, but it became obvious that their way of life was to be destroyed. They were not to dress according to their customs nor to speak their language. Those Gypsies who dealt in the horse trade were hanged if they stole horses. If they were found going about not dressed as *castellanos,* speaking in Gypsy slang, or telling fortunes, they were put in jail. The *Novísima recopilación* made it clear that they had 60 days to live by accepted professions and not become mere vagrants, the next 60 days to leave the realm, and if not, they were subject to 100 lashes, having their ears cut off, 60 days in chains, and exile.

Not all types of work were open to them. Wherever they were, they could only be involved in agriculture or farming. Punishment was dealt out to any Gypsy found on horseback (this may explain why, when offered a horse, Andrés chooses to go on foot: "Levantaron, pues, el rancho, y diéronle a Andrés una pollina en que fuese; pero él no la quiso, sino irse a pie, sirviendo de lacayo a Preciosa" [1: 106]).

The preoccupation with *limpieza de sangre* was extended to the Gypsies, and emigrating to the Indies was equally denied to them, and if found there, they should be removed, because of their ability to deceive the simple and innocent Indians. Punishment for infractions could mean not only hanging but drawing and quartering and being thrown on the byways, with their goods and possessions confiscated.

The only reason for which the Gypsies could leave their ghettos was to work in the fields. Since traditionally or in the past Gypsies were heavily involved in trade of animals, they were prohibited by law from trading major and minor livestock. Gypsies were not allowed to belong to trade guilds, which admitted only *cristianos viejos* (they could join only if they gave up their Gypsy life completely).

Another form of extermination involved separating the Gypsies, breaking them up as a group, especially separating men and women, thereby preventing the continuation of their culture. Children up to the age of ten years were taken away from their parents and educated in the more conventional modes of life, and at ten were put into service as apprentices and taught the Christian life. At the end of the seventeenth century all

Chapter One

Gypsies were assigned residences in particular towns and were submitted to many prohibitions in an attempt to erase their culture.

The Cortes of 1615 and 1617 officially expelled Gypsies from Spain. Expulsion, then, along with internment (as in the case of Jews and Moors, who were confined in *juderías* and *morerías*) became the manner of destroying them. Any Gypsy without a fixed residence and without a profession could be condemned to six years as a galley prisoner. Women (Gypsies or not) who dressed as Gypsies were punished with 100 lashes and banishment. Above all, Gypsies were to give up their weapons. They were made to abandon their ghettos, separated, and assimilated with others where possible. No public assembly of Gypsies was allowed. Yet in spite of whippings, galley punishments, and the threat of the gallows, the Gypsies were known to keep silent under torture.

Looked upon as pariahs, the Gypsies were held responsible for catastrophes, wars, the fall of the Armada, British attacks on Lisbon and La Coruña, the deficit in the treasury, the fall in agricultural production, and the increase in the cost of living. Nevertheless, they survived against all measures and odds. One of their means of survival was to associate themselves with powerful people, who served as sponsors and godparents. The association offered some measure of protection (the above accusations have been culled variously from the sources I have consulted—Clébert, Leblon, Sánchez Ortega, et al.).

By listing all these proscriptions and penalties, the reader no doubt is justified in thinking that no group could possibly have survived such genocidal efforts. It must be said in all fairness that while these prohibitions existed, often either they were not carried out or they were evaded through the skill and duplicity of the Gypsies themselves. What is irrefutable is the atmosphere of intolerance and danger within which the Gypsies lived. "La gitanilla" and Cervantes's *pieza* "Pedro de Urdemalas" are evidence of a public awareness of the presence and lot of Gypsies in Spanish society.

II

Historically, the occupations that seem most associated with Gypsies deal with livestock, mostly horses and mules. This concern is reflected in "La gitanilla." Generally, the Gypsies engaged in horse trading and sales. Documents accused them of stealing the livestock of the poor. Perhaps the meanest and the most effective prohibition by the authorities was to prohibit their activity in the exchange of horses ("haciendo trueques y cambios de cabalgaduras"). (On this subject, see Sánchez Ortega: "Que tampoco puedan tratar en compras, ni venta, ni trueques de animales, ni ganados mayores, ni menores, así en Ferias y Mercados y como fuera de ellos" [52]. See also Covarrubias: "Dezimos a alguno ser gran gitano, quando en el comprar y vender, especialmente bestias, tiene mucha solercia e industria" [643a].) Moncada looked upon all Gypsies as thieves, particularly thieves of animals, livestock being the most common: "Y cuando no pueden robar ganados, procuran engañar con ellos siendo terceros en ferias y mercados" (216). With respect to the involvement of Gypsies with animal life, Leblon notes that "L'histoire de l'âne vendu deux fois, que Berganza raconte dans le *Coloquio,* est un exemple bien choisi des ruses gitanes, également stigmatisées dans *Pedro de Urdemalas*" (*Lit.* 88).[5] Cervantes even goes as far as noting that his Gypsies only steal horses and mules, perhaps reflecting Moncada's negative view of their ruses. Jean-Paul Clébert, in his section "Los gitanos chalanes de caballos," notes that the popular Gypsy saying was not "Le deseo que sea feliz" but rather "Que sus caballos vivan mucho tiempo" (132).

Their entrepreneurial activities were not limited to livestock. Gypsies were also involved in the purchase and sale of fabrics and other merchandise. A popular activity was the telling of fortunes. They also made a practice of begging. They were magicians, trainers of bears, falsifiers, and gamblers, and generally were devoted to the divining arts.

Cervantes was well aware of what the public perception of Gypsies and their lives was, and he brought shades and echoes of this to his narrative.

III

In several documents Gypsies are compared to the two other minorities in Spanish life—Jews and Moors. As a review of history will show, the experiences and tribulations of Gypsies are so reminiscent of the lives led by Jews, *cristianos nuevos,*

Chapter One

and Moors that one can see how Gypsies were classified with these groups. It is Grande who articulates the drama of Gypsies' lives best:

> Los gitanos mezclaron sus músicas y danzas con los de los musulmanes y los judíos no únicamente debido al encuentro peninsular de semejanzas y contactos antiguos y a presumibles raíces comunes en la vieja familia de los siglos, sino también porque, a su llegada a nuestro país, las comunidades perseguidas en él eran la musulmana y la judía. (*Memoria del flamenco* 72)

In fact, the expulsion and diaspora of Gypsies is almost identical to that of Jews. Clébert notes: "Sin embargo, es cierto (y ello es un débil consuelo) que los gitanos, de repente, se desparramaron a través de Oriente, ofreciendo el espectáculo trágico de una dispersión comparable a la diáspora judía"(37). Some even thought that physically there was some resemblance between Jews and Gypsies. Moncada blends both groups together: "y el año de 1568 [el rey] expelió los Judíos dando por razones de su expulsión las que corren en los Gitanos con mayor aprieto" (225–26).

The treatment Gypsies received and the way they were regarded was indicative of the place they occupied in Spain's social and historical structure. The Inquisition did not concern itself with them; they were left to the Santa Hermandad.[6] In 1609, there is expressed the wish for the expulsion of Moors. Gypsies fall into this same category as a detested people.

As stated above, the term *castellanos nuevos* is patterned on *cristianos nuevos,* which designated converted Jews and Moors. "On inventera bientôt un substitut: 'Nouveau-Castillans,' fait sur le modèle de 'Nouveaux Chrétiens' qui désignait jadis les Juifs convertis" (Leblon, *Gitans* 40). The Gypsies were therefore placed in the same category as these other two persecuted groups.[7]

There are several other comparisons that bring these three groups together. All were confined in ghettos where they were forced to live and often prevented from leaving: "Au début du XVIe siècle, on les cantonne dans des sortes de ghettos et on les oblige à porter un signe distinctif, comme l'on a fait au siècle précédent pour les Juifs" (Leblon, *Gitans* 49).[8] The problem of the social marginalization of these groups began with the

Catholic Kings, who had imposed a single authoritarian and absolute view. Whoever did not conform to the official state policy was exiled, destroyed, and exterminated. There was one political, social, and religious standard to be observed.

The ultimate effect of the various prohibitions, pragmatics, and other measures was to destroy the possibilities of a unified national culture and to make of the Gypsies a separate ethnic group: "porque huyen de todo trato con los demás vecinos y prosiguen haciendo como antes su gremio separado, sin aplicarse a oficio o ejercicio honesto ni procurarla a sus hijos" (Sánchez Ortega 169).

The Gypsies were surveilled as the Jews were, especially on the question of marriage. Like the Jews who prepared falsified documents of *hidalguía* in order to live freely in a society governed by the ideal of *cristiandad vieja*, the Gypsies themselves formed close relationships with powerful Christian families and asked them to baptize their children, thereby ensuring some support in a difficult situation.

Focusing on the Moors, Leblon (*Lit.*) comments:

> Les deux races maudites [Gypsies and Moors] sont parfois soumises aux mêmes mesures, car on cherche soit à les assimiler, soit à les expulser, et en tout cas à les faire disparaître en tant que minorité ethnique, particularisme, corps étranger. (183)

But a particularly important and tragically binding similarity occurred in the area of religion and spirituality. Jews and Moors ran afoul of the norms of accepted religion and spirituality; so did the Gypsies, some of whose ideas and practices left the door open to suspicion. Leblon notes: "Un rapport étudié le 8 novembre 1610 affirme que les Gitans ne sont pas chrétiens, puisqu'ils n'observent aucune pratique religieuse, et en conclut qu'ils sont pires que les 'Morisques'" (*Lit.* 167). Keeping in mind their form of life, Leblon remarks:

> La comparaison permanente avec les Morisques, au début du XVIIe siècle, et les préoccupations de l'Espagne au sujet de l'orthodoxie religieuse invitent à penser que les Gitans constituent, en définitive, une sorte de hérésie. "Ces gens là sont bien plus dangereux pour la chrétienté que les Morisques et que toutes les hérésies du passé, car ils s'adressent

Chapter One

davantage au corps qu'à l'esprit" l'écrit Salazar de Mendoza en 1618. (*Gitans* 41)

IV

Cervantes made use of public conceptions of Gypsies in the writing of "La gitanilla." One such conception, their skill at music and dance, was of such importance that the work begins with a musical and choreographical scene.[9] His use of music and dance is more than a merely fanciful one. History shows that Gypsies were closely associated with the world of music, dance, and related endeavors (training of bears, fortune-telling, etc.). Some Gypsy activities became fixed in the popular mind—music and dance were two of these. Cervantes's treatment of this aspect of Gypsy life was conditioned more by life than purely by art:

> Nous venons de voir que, dès le XVIème siècle, les Gitans maquignons et musiciens, et les Gitanes diseuses de bonne aventure et danseuses font partie du folklore et deviennent des personnages familiers pour le public des "autos," et des "comedias." (Leblon, *Lit.* 15)

Grande associated the Gypsy penchant for music and dance with their coequals, Jews and Moors, and adds to this perspective the view that all three groups underwent the same experiences of prejudice, menace, and death. Their music could not help but reflect these experiences, as any listener of the *cante jondo* knows (see Grande, *Memoria del flamenco* 72).

The appearance of Gypsies and aspects of Gypsy life in folklore is further proof of their presence in life. Their music and dance, their use of magic[10] and fortune-telling,[11] all were reflected in the folklore of the times. If Cervantes alluded to amulets in "La gitanilla," it was not an idle gesture, since the use of both amulets and jewels was perceived to be a part of Gypsy life (Clébert 205–06, 225). However, folklore records the Gypsy in lights other than the positive ones (i.e., musicians and dancers). Walter Starkie repeats the popular saying "a gitano, gitano y medio."[12]

The basic plot of "La gitanilla" begins with the notion of the Gypsies as kidnappers, a fear that has lasted on into the twentieth century. The *abuela* says, "que yo la hurté [a Preciosa] en Madrid de vuestra casa el día y hora que ese papel dice" (1: 127). Moncada records that Gypsies were believed to "robar niños y llevarlos a vender en Berbería" (215–16). Preciosa is taken by the old Gypsy woman as a child and reared among the Gypsy tribes. The idea of a Gypsy as a suspicious character who indulged in kidnapping was not lost on a society that expected such behavior.

Kidnapping was only one of the several stereotypes that were held about Gypsies. Cervantes mentioned others elsewhere in the *novela:* "El Alcalde, que estaba presente, comenzó a decir mil injurias a Andrés y a todos los gitanos, llamándolos de públicos ladrones y salteadores de caminos" (1: 124). Similarly the very mention of the word *Gypsy* had to conjure up in the public mind the worst possible pictures. Juana Carducha takes advantage of this bias when she decides to take vengeance on Andrés: "cuando dio voces, diciendo que aquellos gitanos le llevaban robadas sus joyas" (1: 123). Cervantes alternated between the acknowledgment of popular stereotypes about Gypsies and his own questioning of these attitudes by showing that Gypsies can be as good as any non-Gypsy. Expressions of the stereotype abound:

> Parece que los gitanos y gitanas solamente nacieron en el mundo para ser ladrones: nacen de padres ladrones, críanse con ladrones, estudian para ladrones, y, finalmente salen con ser ladrones corrientes y molientes a todo ruedo, y la gana del hurtar y el hurtar son en ellos como ac[c]identes inseparables, que no se quitan sino con la muerte. (1: 61)

> Sucedió, pues, que la mañana de un día que volvían a Madrid a coger la garrama con las demás gitanillas. . . . (1: 83)

> y lo que es más, que la crianza tosca en que se criaba no descubría en ella [Preciosa] sino ser nacida de mayores prendas que de gitana, porque era en extremo cortés y bien razonada. (1: 62)

> Una, pues, desta nación, gitana vieja, que podía ser jubilada en la ciencia de Caco, crió una muchacha en nombre de nieta suya, a quien puso [por] nombre Preciosa y a quien enseñó todas sus gitanerías, y modos de embelecos, y trazas de hurtar. (1: 61)

Chapter One

> En el tiempo que él faltó dió cuenta Preciosa a su madre de todo el discurso de su vida, y de como siempre había creído ser gitana y ser nieta de aquella vieja; pero que siempre se había estimado en mucho más de lo que de ser gitana se esperaba. (1: 131)

Other passages show the better side of the Gypsies: "Veníos con nosotros, que, aunque somos gitanos, no lo parecemos en la caridad" (1: 108); "Llegóse a él Andrés y otro gitano caritativo—que aun entre los demonios hay unos peores que otros, y entre muchos malos hombres suele haber alguno bueno . . ." (1: 109). Cervantes even created a situation that would probably have been very unlikely in life—the lieutenant asks the Gypsies to go to his home: "y habiéndole parecido por todo extremo bien la gitanilla, mandó a un paje suyo dijese a la gitana vieja que al anochecer fuese a su casa con las gitanillas" (1: 71).

It is from both these sources, history (reality) and folkore, that Gypsy life is channeled into literature. In composing "La gitanilla," Cervantes astutely availed himself of those aspects of Gypsy folklore that had permeated everyday life in Spain.

V

Leblon, in both his excellent works, meaningfully suggests a motivation for Cervantes that must be considered seriously. He notes that "La gitanilla" and "Coloquio de los perros" (where other facets of Gypsy culture are treated) frame the collection of tales. The reality of the Gypsy lifestyle was well known to Cervantes; perhaps he was attracted to the myth of freedom that was associated with it,[13] but in redoing this way of life in literature, Cervantes added to it values that perhaps Gypsies did not entirely possess. What is produced, according to Leblon, is a "jeu littéraire" that becomes a burlesque representation of Gypsy life (see *Lit.* 203 ff.). According to Leblon:

> L'évasion dans le "gitanisme" n'est réalisable que si les Gitans sont traités comme un thème littéraire; et leur idéalisation est rendue possible parce-qu'il s'agit d'un monde à part qui s'oppose un monde réel dans lequel Cervantes est contraint de vivre non plus dans le temps, comme la Chevalerie ou l'Age d'or, mais dans le présent, grâce à leur vie

de parias, d'asociaux, de marginaux, parce qu'ils constituent un monde différent, isolé et mystérieux. (*Lit.* 203)[14]

For Leblon, Cervantes's creative act—i.e., the creation of the literary Gypsy—is a form of writing, "une évasion, et un constat d'échec" (*Lit.* 201). All Cervantes's literature is a "littérature de l'échec" (201). Of particular interest to me is Leblon's belief that Cervantes introduced the "douloureuse confrontation, en introduisant le réel dans la fiction, ou la fiction dans le réel" (201). While I am in agreement with Leblon on some of his ideas here, I do not think that literature, Cervantes's or anyone else's, must be a "littérature de l'echec." Cervantes's audacity in presenting society with an idealized picture of a marginal minority group is for me a positive and creative gesture. His art is more than any mere mimesis of reality.

Preciosa's maturity and depth of wisdom belie her 15 years. Her depiction in every sense belongs to an ideal feminine picture, just as the depiction of Andrés Caballero responds to the creation of another ideal type. Andrés is, as far as the creation of Cervantes is concerned, one of the "gitanos de honor," as Clébert calls them (159). His behavior as a *gitano* defies other popular concepts and views of Gypsies. The text testifies to the idealized character of the couple:

> —Yo, señor caballero, aunque soy gitana pobre y humildemente nacida, tengo un cierto espiritillo fantástico acá dentro, que a grandes cosas me lleva. . . . Una sola joya tengo, que la estimo en más que a la vida, que es la de mi entereza y virginidad. (1: 85)

> – Si quisiéredes ser mi esposo, yo lo seré vuestra; pero han de preceder muchas condiciones y averiguaciones primero. (1: 86)

> —No todas somos malas—respondió Preciosa—. . . . Y vámonos, abuela, que aquí nos tienen en poco. ¡Pues en verdad que no somos ladronas ni rogamos a nadie!
> —No os enojéis, Preciosa—dijo el padre—; que, a lo menos de vos, imagino que no se puede presumir cosa mala; que vuestro buen rostro os acredita y sale por fiador de vuestras buenas obras. Por vida de Preciosita que bailéis un poco con vuestras compañeras. (1: 95)

Chapter One

> Pasaba Andrés con Preciosa honestos, discretos y enamorados coloquios, y ella poco a poco se iba enamorando de la discreción y buen trato de su amante, y él, del mismo modo, si pudiera crecer su amor, fuera creciendo: tal era la honestidad, discreción y belleza de su Preciosa. (1: 107–08)

> —No os turbéis; animaos, y no penséis que habéis llegado a un pueblo de ladrones, sino a un asilo que os sabrá guardar y defender de todo el mundo. (1: 112)

Even Andrés's expressions of idealism are a part of the general schema that Cervantes has presented in support of Gypsies:

> —Yo no la pretendo para burlalla, ni en las veras del amor que la tengo puede caber género de burla alguna; sólo quiero servirla del modo que ella más gustare: su voluntad es la mía. (1: 84)

> [Andrés] defraudó las esperanzas que sus padres en él tenían, dejó el camino de Flandes, donde había de ejercitar el valor de su persona y acrecentar la honra de su linaje, y se vino a postrarse a los pies de una muchacha, y a ser su lacayo, que, puesto que hermosísima, en fin, era gitana: privilegio de la hermosura, que trae al redopelo y por la melena a sus pies a la voluntad más exenta. (1: 106)

Andrés's adopted name, "Caballero," is a clever manipulation on the part of Cervantes. It represents a commentary on Andrés's background, as well as an ironic acknowledgment of the possibility that such a concept could be applied to a Gypsy (when Andrés takes the name "Caballero" the text reads: "porque también había gitanos entre ellos deste apellido" [1: 90]; and later Andrés swears, "que yo os prometo por la fe de caballero gitano" [1: 112]).

Cervantes discarded all the negative stereotypes, and ended up creating Gypsy characters that, while not conforming particularly to contemporary views, are, in the words of Agustín González de Amezúa y Mayo, "gitanos corteses, humanos, tratables y generosos" (2: 11). Cervantes's artistic invention representaba a blatant rejection of the picture commonly held of Gypsies, both men and women.

In a series of observations, Jennifer Lowe supports the literary creative aspect of the work when she points to the fact that the dénouement is telegraphed early in the *novela* by showing that the *abuela* is not Preciosa's true grandmother (28). Her purpose, if I understand Lowe correctly, would have to be to focus on what Cervantes does with the fictional world that he creates as well as its affective quality as art. This is made more obvious when she observes that the society of Gypsies in the work is questionable (38). Even Andrés's crime—murder—must then be seen as a literary *inventio,* for, in the process, he neither gets hanged nor loses honor (45). Therefore his continuation in the *novela* can be seen as functioning only within a literary purview.

In this case Cervantes adopts the real-life concerns of individuals who give up their lives to follow the pull of idealized lifestyles, among them, the Gypsy life. According to Luis Rosales, Cervantes took some real aspects of life and joined them to a created world conditioned by artistic demands. The characters were attracted by the *convivencia* with nature, nomadic Gypsy life, and the "convención de la vida social."[15] In their ideal tracings, the characters, as far as historical fact is concerned, represent the opposite or the unexpected. They defy some of the stereotypes that were commonly held at the time. This, then, becomes a vehicle for Cervantes's "prise de conscience" of a thoroughly unethical and immoral situation (the condition and treatment of Gypsies) rather than an "acte révolutionnaire."[16] It is another example of the same situation with Jews and Moors. The comparison between Gypsies and the other two groups, already well known and understood in his society, could not have gone unperceived in this tale. Cervantes's artistry did not idly embellish reality; it also emphasized its pain.

VI

In his effort to prove the Counter-Reformation background and features of *Las novelas ejemplares,* Casalduero notes that in "La gitanilla,"

> lo que sentimos es la profunda emoción religiosa de la Contrarreforma, que permite concebir al hombre en toda su dignidad racional instituyendo sobre la libertad de la naturaleza, una libertad superior, de un orden maravillosamente inflexible, que encuadra rígidamente la esencia de las cosas: la libertad de la gracia divina.[17]

Chapter One

Casalduero's view seems to be ponderous for a work whose purpose, it seems to me, is to function seriously but on a less profound plane that he supposes. But in spite of Casalduero's usually authoritative point of view, I contend that part of the backlash that society had toward Gypsies was conditioned by attitudes toward some of their religious practices. Leblon cites Moncada, who fulminates against them:

> Lo sexto, porque muy graves hombres los tienen por Hereges, i muchos por Gentiles, Idólatras y Ateos, sin religión alguna, aunque en la apariencia exterior se acomodan con la religión de la Provincia donde andan, siendo con los Turcos Turcos, con los Hereges Hereges, i entre christianos bautizando algún muchacho por cumplir. (Moncada 217, cited by Leblon, *Lit.* 168)

The Gypsies were looked upon like the Moors, whose customs conflicted with accepted practices of religion. Like the Moors they were not baptized and did not marry according to Christian rites. Even a century later as Sánchez Ortega cites, the Gypsies were accused of "haciendo mil insultos, viviendo con poco temor de Dios, y sin ser Cristianos, más que en el nombre" (135). Complaints about them are recorded in the Cortes of 1603, in which it is asserted "qu'ils vivent 'sans l'entière connaissance de la loi chrétienne'" (cited by Leblon, *Lit.* 167).[18] Clébert, on the other hand, notes that the Gypsies always adapted themselves to the prevalent religious practices,[19] but they were reluctant to marry according to accepted church practices, thereby rejecting that religion; this is one of the biggest complaints about them. That Cervantes opposes such a view is supported by the treatment that is given in the text to the attitudes of Gypsies toward marriage (Leblon, *Gitans* 45–46): "Sosiega, sosiega, alborotadito, y mira lo que haces primero que te cases, y danos una limosnita por Dios y por quien tú eres" (1: 94). Andrés voices this position when, to fend off Juana Carducha, he reminds her of the mores to which he has pledged himself: "—Señora doncella, yo estoy apalabrado para casarme, y los gitanos no nos casamos sino con gitanas" (1: 122). Much has been made of the reluctance of the priest to marry Preciosa and Andrés because the banns had not been announced. This seems very shaky. In a culture in which many "sacred" religious values

"La gitanilla"

are conveniently dispensed with, could it be that the priest, accustomed to being wary about Gypsies and their own sets of values about marriage, not to mention the general caution people had about them, is *afraid* to marry them unconditionally and without a clarification of their situation?

> —Señor tiniente cura, este gitano y esta gitana son los que vuesa merced ha de desposar.
> —Eso no podré yo hacer si no preceden primero las circunstancias que para tal caso se requieren. ¿Dónde se han hecho las amonestaciones? ¿Adónde está la licencia de mi superior, para que con ella se haga el desposorio? (1: 132)

Leblon also notes that many Gypsies are born in the woods and the country and, because of the possible inaccessibility of churches or because of strong clannish feelings, probably did not have their children baptized. Keeping in mind Casalduero's remarks stated above, the Gypsies ignored the church practices and views, including "recent" Counter-Reformation decrees on marriage (Leblon, *Gitans* 52). In essence, while marriage is a social act, Casalduero notes that it is filled with religious spirit, "Honestidad y matrimonio tridentino" (52, 53). Forcione sees the refusal to perform the marriage without the banns as a reflection of reformist thinking in marriage (156–57). These views can be compared with that of Leblon:

> Les espagnols du XVIIème siècle ne connaissent qu'une sorte de mariage: c'est le sacrement administré par l'Eglise. Or, de tous temps, les Gitans ont célébré leurs mariages selon leurs propres coutumes. Ils ont eu, presque toujours, un certain mépris pour le mariage religieux que Cervantes désigne ici (*Lit.* 170; see also Laspéras on marriage and the Counter-Reformation)

Perhaps even more serious for their relations with Christian life, Gypsies, according to Leblon, died without sacraments and did not demand church burial (see *Gitans* 52). The Gypsies' adherence to clan mores and a rejection of the consecrated practices of the church, especially those regarding Christian marriage and death, caused the authorities and the general public to view them as heretics, and this perception could only intensify the prejudice that was held against them.

Chapter One

Given Preciosa's concern about marriage, it is worth examining more deeply some Gypsy attitudes and those of the society at large in order to understand better why Cervantes chose this theme for his *novela*. However, it becomes obvious that with respect to the institution of marriage, the history of Gypsy life reveals some inconsistencies with Cervantes's text. Andrés's love for, and marriage to, Preciosa is out of the ordinary. As Clébert states,

> porque, para que un *gachó* se convierta realmente en un gitano, debería, por lo menos, casarse con una gitana. Y el matrimonio entre gitanos y no gitanos está formalmente reprobado. La mayoría de las veces lleva consigo la exclusión de la tribu, y el proscrito no tiene ya derecho al nombre de gitano (Es indiferente que sea hombre o mujer el que contraiga "injustas" nupcias). Algunas veces, este ostracismo se extiende a toda su familia y a la descendencia del culpable. (159)

Furthermore, Clébert continues (160), "una ley implacable prohíbe todo matrimonio fuera de este grupo," or even "No le será posible, por ejemplo, casarse con una gitana ni tener descendencia con derecho a ese nombre" (158). The trial and marriage of Andrés, as an outsider, to Preciosa could not probably have taken place in reality. Andrés Caballero's whole episode as a "fellow traveling" Gypsy was a very risky endeavor. Numerous Cortes actions prohibit such playacting (see above). In this respect see also Moncada: "Y que no puedan usar del traje, lengua, y nombre de Gitanos y Gitanas, sino que pues no lo son de nación, quede perpetuamente este nombre y uso confundido y olvidado" (222).[20] The social prohibitions concerning the possible marriage are of course all too easily resolved at the end when it is learned that Preciosa is not a bona fide Gypsy but a social equal of Andrés. But this fortuitous resolution happens only at the end. The "affair" between Andrés and Preciosa represents for me an imaginative excursus into the realm of dreams: Andrés's, to break with convention and go off and join a prohibited social minority; Preciosa's, to test this dream flight by placing in Andrés's way obstacles to be overcome. Andrés's adventure is an experience of vicarious living in a way of life detested by his own social class. At the end you have two Christians who will embark upon a Christian marriage and follow the path of Christian living.[21] All prohibitions have become void. But it is undeniable that Cervantes's portrayal of idealized femininity in Preciosa brings to the Christian readership a sympathetic picture of Gypsy life. It represents a type of reverse idealism[22] in which Cervantes indulges by portraying a detested group in the same moral, positive terms as the Christians, a daring act indeed. This is further intensified by Andrés, who willingly gives up his life as a young Spanish "nobleman," who abandons everything to join a way of life seen by that same Spanish society in such negative terms. Cervantes solves the problem of possible social revolution (i.e., the rejection of Spanish mores and inclusion in the society of Gypsies) by undoing Preciosa's status as bona fide Gypsy,[23] thereby choosing the retention of the status quo over the unlikely and the romantic.

VII

The primacy of Preciosa as a character of this work necessitates an analysis of public attitudes toward Gypsy women. Preciosa is well known for her vocal and dancing abilities (see above note 9), and the public associated Gypsies with music and dance. Clébert quotes Father Mariana, who, in his *Tratado contra los juegos públicos,* notes, "condenaba al infierno las *zarabandas* tan lascivas en palabras, tan odiosas en sus movimientos que hacen ruborizar a las personas honestas" (150–51). The text states: "que no consentía Preciosa que las que fuesen en su compañía cantasen cantares descompuestos" (1: 66). There is no hint in Preciosa's dancing and singing of what Father Mariana describes, but the very presence of a dancing Gypsy girl must have conjured up in the popular mind numerous images and expectations (see above for Moncada's observation regarding Gypsy women; see also Leblon, *Lit.* 169). On the other hand, Clébert informs us that one of the worst "crimes" in Gypsy life is for a woman to be a prostitute. Prostitution would exclude a woman from the tribe. A woman might give herself over in love to someone, but public prostitution of the type Moncada describes (215) is definitely rejected in Gypsy life. Leblon also quotes an effort to rid Spanish society of Gypsy

Chapter One

women by sending nubile ones to Latin America to be married off to Indians (see *Gitans* 66; see also Wilson, who suggests an interesting connection between Gypsies and Amerindians). This is another manner of eradicating the Gypsies by exile and dispersion.

Another feature of marriage that Starkie notes would accord with Preciosa's project of marriage to Andrés. Submitting to a process of testing and approval, Andrés attaches himself to the Gypsy tribe as a Gypsy and is assimilated into the group (see 339). Preciosa's oft-quoted passage regarding the importance of virginity must have come as a brutal surprise to individuals who held Father Mariana's view of Gypsy women. The important stress by Preciosa of her virginity recalls the theme in Golden Age *comedias*. We may have here Cervantes's reaction once again to Lopean dramaturgy or even in a reactive way to many a picaresque heroine (on this last point see Lowe 52). In the "Gypsy period" of Preciosa's life, she is the hallmark of honesty, purity, innocence, and steadfastness. Once again, Cervantes idealizes for us a debased aspect of Gypsy life. El Saffar notes that "Nobility is the label Cervantes applies to a condition achieved on *a posteriori* through, and as a result of, struggle" (*Novel to Romance* 26). She also points out an ironic touch in the reversal motif:

> With this discovery [the dénouement] the story turns full-circle from the beginning: it is now Preciosa who is of noble blood and who is obedient to her parents yet secretly in love with Andrés; and it is Andrés who appears to be nothing but a Gypsy. (98)

Forcione provides valuable insight with respect to the view of society that the work includes:

> Defined in opposition to the conventional order, the Gypsy society provides a moral standard against which ceremonialism, corruption, flattery, distrust, greed, and other abuses which afflict the "civilized" society of contemporary Spain can be clarified by contrast and condemned. (186)

VIII

Preciosa as a typical Golden Age character is subject to all the rules governing women in a situation of *honra*. Like Lope,

"La gitanilla"

Cervantes could not ignore the mandates of this social issue and thus assimilates its concern into the story, as is witnessed by several *novelas* dealing with the theme (see below chapter 4, "The Prose of Honor").

However, while Cervantes paid homage to the demands of the honor theme, he subverted it by portraying a Gypsy society that had abandoned most of conventional society's values, including *honra*. The speech by the old Gypsy is a paean to a society untouched by concerns such as *honra;* it is a society devoid of *melindres . . . muchas cerimonias* (1: 101), and since it comes out of the mouth of a pariah, it can be seen as the viewpoint of the dominant society. If the dominant society had rejected Gypsies and had tried to exterminate them, the Gypsies in turn had rejected the values of that same dominant society.

Cervantes structures a situation that will examine the dominant value of nobility (and *honra*). During a considerable part of the story the theme of *honra* comes forth as a major concern of the tale, with *sangre noble* being examined indirectly and put to the test in this plot. Andrés does not really lose any honor by joining the Gypsy band, since it is done within a "playful" vein. Preciosa stands to increase her honor, since she will not betray her standards of conduct by losing her virginity to a person of superior social class. The steadfastness of the couple will affirm their quality even more, and since one of the parties is not socially acceptable, the conventional social criteria by which they are judged are then brought into question.

Franz Rauhut (150) points out cogently: "La nobleza, que ya no tenía derechos políticos, necesitaba tanto más la creencia en la sangre noble que se hereda con todas las cualidades aristocráticas." Preciosa's father becomes the representative of the old view of *honra*. In the final analysis, Cervantes is suggesting the hazardous notion that true *honra* and nobility must be revealed in one's actions, not in one's titles or social standing. Even Andrés's blatant murder of the official does not tarnish his personal *honra*. The dénouement of the tale represents Cervantes's guarded and cautious resolution. His art is to reveal, tempt, criticize, but in the end he retreats. Preciosa is really of noble blood, which saves Andrés from the certain social ignominy of his fully having joined the Gypsy band and becoming a Gypsy.

Chapter One

On the one hand, as Leblon (*Lit.* 195) states with respect to Cervantes:

> Ainsi, face à une société hypocrite et corrompue, basée, sur des fausses valeurs telles que "honra," "linaje," "limpieza de sangre," etc., le monde libre des Gitans nous offrirait tout un choix de vertus authentiques: fidélité, fraternité, loyauté, courage, sagesse. . . . Que Cervantes ait pu souffrir de ces fausses valeurs sociales c'est certain. On peut souligner: *Ni madrugamos a dar memoriales, ni a acompañar magnates, ni a solicitar favores* [emphasis in original].[24]

Is the suggestion of Cervantes's betrayal of a strong position on *honra* and *linaje* a fair one? The handling of the case of Ricote the Moor in *Don Quijote* is similar; Cervantes masks the situation of all *cristianos* (and *castellanos?*) *nuevos* behind the figure of Ricote the Moor.[25] It is difficult to ignore the meaning of Ricote's plight and Cervantes's position, just as in "La gitanilla" (and other *novelas*) Cervantes's position on the vacuity of *honra* is clear. In "La gitanilla" Cervantes served a double purpose: to expose the vacuity of the concept of *honra* and to examine and reveal the inhumane treatment of one of Spain's minorities. Cervantes availed himself of an age-old literary topos (Heliodorus) and recast it in a new, contemporary context of cruelty, prejudice, and bias. One must not overlook the theory of Forcione concerning this tale: "*La Gitanilla* is a tale of courtship and rational wedded love, and its plot depicts the formation of a perfect family in the union of Juan and Preciosa" (95). While there are many perceptive insights in his interpretation of this tale, for me the overwhelming historical documentation indicates that the focus of the tale is the social and historical condition of Gypsies rather than the theme of ideal marriage.

IX

It has been a matter of curiosity as to why in "La gitanilla" Cervantes used no *caló;* there are no signs of Gypsy slang either. Moncada calls attention to the Gypsies' use of *jerigonza* as a warning to unwary people that might come into contact with them (218). Covarrubias has an interesting insight into Gypsy speech:

> Y la lengua que hablan propia tira a la esclavona; no embargante que tengan otra ficticia con que se entienden, que

"La gitanilla"

> comúnmente llamamos gerigonça, corrompido el vocablo de zingerionza, lenguaje de cíngaros. Estos deprenden fácilmente la lengua de la provincia por donde passan, y assí saben muchas. (642b)

Although there are examples of the use of *jerigonza* in "Pedro de Urdemalas," its absence in "La gitanilla" merely attracts attention to itself. Cervantes knew *germanía* but reveals no examples or knowledge of *caló*. While there is no example of the use of *caló*, we do have an example of an analogous form of Andalusian speech, which may be the closest that Cervantes comes to Gypsy speech in "La gitanilla": "—¿Quiérenme dar barato, ceñores?—dijo Preciosa, que, como gitana, hablaba ceceoso" (1: 72). Another reason for the absence of Gypsy speech may be that Gypsies did not use it in their social intercourse with others. Perhaps Cervantes avoided use of *caló* because of the official prohibition against the use of the Gypsies' language (see above). It is tempting to think that Cervantes was well aware of such prohibitions and saw them as basically unfair, because they further despoiled the Gypsies of their identity and individuality. If Cervantes had shown the characters speaking *caló*, he might also have run the risk of allowing the story to fall into a kind of benign *costumbrismo*,[26] which would have blunted his attack on the official position toward the Gypsies as a minority group in Spain at that time.

X

Michael Gerli suggests that the major themes of "La gitanilla" are not life, marriage, and constancy, but "moral freedom, spiritual nobility and honor based on the observance of Christian principles and the exercise of conscience" (31). Each *novela* has the potential for offering a moral suggestion. Lowe suggests that the exemplarity is fundamental to the story. It is a "successful combination of 'ejercicios honestos y agradables' and 'ejemplo provechoso'" (Lowe 55). The thrust, as I have suggested earlier, is an historical, contemporaneous "prise de conscience" on the part of a benevolent and humanitarian Cervantes. Any possible exemplarity would be submerged beneath a larger "morality" (or immorality) of the conflict expressed by the figure of Preciosa and the group to which she belongs. It is a state even more severe than fights between the

Chapter One

Montagues and the Capulets. We have here one huge sector of Spanish life rising up against a smaller group of people who are marginal and marginalized members of that same society.

In spite of the title of the collection and the claims that Cervantes made of adhering to a principle of the exemplarity of literature, I see these as mere lip service to a commonly accepted rhetorical principle that Cervantes used in a somewhat subversive way.

XI

Cervantes strove for a linguistic balance between a naturalistic presentation and one in which the consciousness of verbal handling as art is present. He did the same with the atmosphere of his work. José María Chacón y Calvo would have us believe that the first words of the story "ya envuelven al lector en este ambiente de la concreta y precisa realidad" (248), which echoes Francisco A. de Icaza's view that "los detalles de época son de una observación justa y de una exactitud indiscutible" (130). But as Gerli points out, this idealism is a manifestation of a deeper problem. He sees a "surface idealism checked by a subterfuge of irony which establishes a more realistic and essentially ambiguous vision of events" (30). This would tend to support my view of the historical dimensions of the tale. The "ideal world" that Cervantes created is itself a deception, inasmuch as he hints at a deeper conflict, orienting the reader toward it with pointed signs. The "ideality" of the story comes crashing down with, among other things, the episode of la Carducha, in which a murder takes place and the possibility of Andrés's guilt and hanging stands as a very real consequence of his actions.

Cervantes's skill was unsurpassable inasmuch as he created a second reality, a literary one, removed from the sordid, ugly reality that was attached to the lives and mores of Gypsies. His scope was very far reaching. The depiction of Preciosa's parents cuttingly shows in the moral dichotomy in Preciosa's life, her moral solidness as opposed to the "ignominious reality" of her parents' empty respectability (Gerli 33). In this way Cervantes does not have to lay claim to having created a completely imagined or imaginative situation. His skill depends on his ability to deal successfully with the ideal and the real

"La gitanilla"

worlds. As Dunn says: "el idilio está deliberadamente colocado en un mundo naturalista (gitano, ladrones . . .) para poder trascenderlo" (91). To be sure, Cervantes was aware of the brutal and sordid treatment afforded to Gypsies. As Manuel López Rodríguez states:

> De una u otra forma, lo que sí es seguro es que cuando Cervantes empezó a escribir, el mundo de los gitanos era ya sobradamente conocido en España, lo suficiente como para que una mente curiosa y clara como la suya pudiese llevar a sus páginas los rasgos más sobresalientes de aquel elemento humano. (13)[27]

In "La gitanilla," then, which opens the collection of *novelas*, Cervantes makes a very strong statement about cruelty, narrowness of vision, closure of mind, and the place for compassion and understanding toward individuals whose lives are different from that of the average Spaniard.

Chapter Two

Católicos secretos, Conversos, and the Myth of the Maritime Life in "La española inglesa"

I

In keeping with the interpretation that I have given to "La gitanilla" (and as I shall do with other stories), I see in "La española inglesa" an example of Cervantes's historical, religious, and social sensitivity to his time and his wish to interpret critically certain events to his fellow Spaniards through his writing.

In a tersely argued essay, Carroll B. Johnson advanced an interpretation of "La española inglesa" in which he asserts that the text is filled with "real historical and social issues" and studies how it passes into a literary format ("'La española inglesa'" 379). Basically, Johnson focuses on the year 1605 as a key to understanding a series of historical and economic events and goes on to show how these historical and economic factors condition the creation of Cervantes's tale.[1]

The scope of my historical and political view goes well beyond Johnson's insistence on the second siege of Cádiz. Accordingly, I shall build my analysis around what I see as three coordinated points in the discourse: the phrase *católicos secretos* as a key to one important part of the action; the allusion to the siege of Cádiz as a general reference that links with the failure of the Armada and the earlier successful English attack on Cádiz under Sir Francis Drake; and the myth of the maritime life and concept of freedom that this myth signifies.

II

The phrase *católicos secretos* stands out in the beginning of the tale as a clear signal of one of the most important strands of the historical background and content of the tale. This strand is the conflict between the followers of Elizabeth and the

39

Chapter Two

Anglican church and the recusant Catholics of sixteenth- and seventeenth-century England (cf. "Quiso la buena suerte que todos los de la casa de Clotaldo eran católicos secretos, aunque en lo público mostraban seguir la opinión de su reina" [1: 244]).

The first historical clue given to the reader is reference to the siege of Cádiz in 1596 under the command of the Earl of Essex[2] and Lord Howard. Another is the problem of recusancy and Catholic practice and adherence that goes back even earlier than 1596 (or 1603 or 1605, as Johnson insists). The situation of recusancy is a step along the way between the reign of Mary Tudor (1553–58) and 1603, the year of the death of Elizabeth Tudor and the accession by James I to the throne. The problem of *católicos secretos* is also an historical one, and the history of Catholic recusancy is linked with Philip II of Spain, although his name is not mentioned in this tale.

The marriage of Mary Tudor to Philip II led to a certain instability in relations between England and Spain. Such a marriage was not viewed as an auspicious event and led to the fear that England would be returning to the influence of the Pope (Campbell 2). The view that Philip was working hand in glove with the Pope was not an idle one; it was certainly in the best interests of the Papacy to have as austere a Catholic as Philip II in power, but in spite of this warranted supposition, the historical developments in England showed that while English Catholics were loyal to their religion, they were not so loyal to extraterritorial politics (i.e., Spain's politics). A concomitant fear created by this union was that England could be invaded by Spain, unlikely as that may have seemed.[3] Such a fear tended to be used to justify allegiance to Elizabeth.[4]

If the situation of secret Catholics and their persecution in sixteenth-century England elicited a strong response by Catholics, a similar situation existed about 1554, when English Catholics persecuted Protestants. In her efforts to return England to the Catholic Church, Mary had identified "Catholicism with the burning of heretics and the influence of Spain" (Morey 20). Alison Plowden succinctly describes the meaning of this marriage:

> Mary Tudor's politically disastrous Spanish marriage, coinciding as it did with one of England's periodic attacks of

xenophobia, had polluted the whole of her regime with the taint of foreign interference and oppression. Fairly or unfairly, Roman Catholicism was not to lose that taint for centuries. (34)

There were other causes that created this anti-Catholic situation in England. On Christmas Day, 1558, Elizabeth I ordered that the Host not be elevated at High Mass, a command that Owen Oglethorp, Bishop of Carlisle, rejected. Elizabeth then forbade all preaching and teaching: "gospel, epistle and ten commandments were to be recited in the vernacular 'without exposition or addition'" (Plowden 25). Such an edict could only alienate what there was of a Catholic hierarchy and laity, and proved to be a harbinger of worse things to come. In April 1559, Elizabeth invoked the Act of Supremacy ("It repealed Mary's Catholic legislation and designated Elizabeth as supreme governor of the church" [Campbell 3]). There were *in toto* two Acts of Supremacy and Uniformity enacted that forced Catholics to acknowledge Elizabeth Tudor as head of the Church and State and the Anglican rite as the authorized form of religious expression. Naturally, these edicts forced a choice upon Catholics that they could not accept. Plowden notes that "Anyone who refused to take the Oath of Supremacy was deprived of office and barred from holding office for life." A number of other punishments were prescribed as well (49–50), as will become evident in the study of Catholic recusants that follows.

Elizabeth's edicts did not go without a response from the Papacy, for in 1570 Pope Pius V promulgated the bull *Regnans in Excelsis,* which called for the excommunication of Elizabeth I. Essentially, the bull made Elizabeth "'a heretic and a fautor of heretics'" (Watkin 27). The political interplay between Elizabeth's edicts and the Pope's bull created the atmosphere of direct persecution and response that was responsible for much of the negative and destructive spirit between Catholics and Protestants at that time. The papal bull not only excommunicated Elizabeth but also declared her deposed, and, of particular interest to my thesis, her subjects were absolved of their oaths of allegiance. If the Catholics were suspect, it was not without some good reason. Killing in the name of the church or some church principle, i.e., regicide, was not out of the question.

Chapter Two

But there were other underlying causes of the hostility between Elizabeth and Philip (or, put another way, between England and Spain). The first half of the sixteenth century involves a number of religious questions often intimately associated with political ones. In the very active pirating and privateering atmosphere in the Mediterranean and the West Indies, plunder "increasingly identified itself with Protestantism and patriotism" (Andrews 15). This attitude may be a product of a similar one on the part of Spain and Catholics. The Armada was not without its messianic and religious interpreters in Spain and was generally looked upon as a religious crusade against Protestants.

Casalduero's interpretation of "La española inglesa" asserts that Cervantes's critical focus is not Protestants or Protestantism: "Apenas se hace alusión al protestantismo, y cuando se le alude se le trata desde un punto de vista social (al querer justificar el envenenamiento de Isabel)" (97). The critical attitude of the work, according to Casalduero, is more precisely focused on Catholics: "El enemigo no es Inglaterra, ni siquiera el protestante, sino el católico tibio. Esto es, el enemigo del hombre es el propio hombre. Quien roba a Isabel no es un protestante—el conde de Essex—, sino un católico tibio: Clotaldo" (102). He continues:

> Cervantes está expresando, dando forma, a esa esperanza, que por tanto tiempo sintió la España filipina, de ver a los católicos tibios de Inglaterra volver la hija a sus padres, el Alma al Santo Padre, de ingresar de nuevo en el seno de un catolicismo sin mancha.... El significado de la novela, pues, parece surgir claramente si vemos, junto y sobre la escala mística que recorre el hombre individual para llegar a la total unión, el sacudimiento de toda tibieza en el católico y la depuración de su religión, tan tristemente mezclada con escorias. Cervantes se eleva a una zona verdaderamente mística para dar forma a un problema político que en España aparecía con carácter religioso. (103)

Like Casalduero, I believe that the focus of the work is on Catholics, which, of course, implicates Protestants and the problem of religious autonomy and control as manipulated by Elizabeth and her ministers against Catholics, Rome, and particularly

Católicos secretos

in this case, Philip II, and possibly Philip III. Kenneth R. Andrews offers a valuable insight into this view: "Their motives were mixed: some, like Walsingham, who sponsored Drake's South Seas venture, the Terceira project and Fenton's voyage, as well as less aggressive enterprises, were moved chiefly by hostility to Spain and Roman Catholicism" (18).

Many efforts were geared at destroying the Catholic faith and its adherents during Elizabeth's reign. One of the greatest fears was of a Catholic invasion of England, an idea that was broached by Philip II and his advisors more than once. Such an invasion could, with the assistance and blessing of the Papacy, have returned Catholicism to England.[5] This view was espoused by such Catholics as Dr. William Allen and Robert Persons (as reported by Norman 18). Cervantes's text should guide us as to the presence and meaning of this difficult religious situation. From the very beginning we are made aware of the problem by Cervantes's reference to the characters as *católicos secretos*. The word *secreto* occurs again when we are told, "aunque iba aprendiendo la lengua inglesa, no perdía la española, porque Clotaldo [Ricaredo's father and Isabel's kidnapper] tenía cuidado de traerle a casa *secretamente* [emphasis mine] españoles que hablasen con ella" (1: 244). The "Catholicity" of the action is further intensified by noting that Ricaredo was promised to a Scottish woman "asimismo *secreta* [emphasis mine] cristiana como ellos" (1: 245).

This secret Catholic group is characterized by the tension and awareness of functioning in a clandestine way: Ricaredo's mother, Catalina, says: "—¡Ay . . . si sabe la reina que yo he criado a esta niña a la católica, y de aquí viene a inferir que todos los desta casa somos cristianos!" (1: 247). Another reference cues the reader further as to the secretive nature of the Catholic family. After a note arrives from the Queen, we are told: "Discurrieron aquella noche en muchas cosas, especialmente en que si la reina supiera que eran católicos no les enviara recaudo tan manso" (1: 248). Catholic custom and presence is further observed by Ricaredo when he avers: "—Si me das la palabra de ser mía, yo te la doy, desde luego, como verdadero y católico cristiano, de ser tuyo; que puesto que no llegue a gozarte, como no llegaré, hasta que con bendición de la Iglesia y de mis padres sea" (1: 245). All of Ricaredo's actions involve

Chapter Two

a tremendous loyalty to his clandestine religion. After Ricaredo's ship is captured, the narrator wonders:

> si [Ricaredo] había de responder a su católico intento, que le impedía no desenvainar la espada contra católicos. . . . Pero, en fin, determinó de posponer al gusto de enamorado el que tenía de ser católico, y en su corazón pedía al cielo le deparase ocasiones donde, con ser valiente, cumpliese con ser cristiano, dejando a su reina satisfecha y a Isabel merecida. (1: 252)

In another passage we read:

> de que recibió gran gusto Ricaredo, pareciéndole que aquella presa, si el cielo se la concediese, sería de consideración, sin haber ofendido a ningún católico. Las dos galeras turquescas llegaron a reconocer los navíos ingleses, los cuales no traían insignias de Inglaterra, sino de España. (1: 253)

And:

> Y así, soy de parecer que ningún cristiano católico muera; no porque los quiero bien, sino porque me quiero a mí muy bien, y querría que esta hazaña de hoy ni a mí ni a vosotros, que en ella me habéis sido compañeros, nos diese, mezclado con el nombre de valientes, el renombre de crueles. (1: 256)

Cervantes complicates the situation by having Ricaredo identify with perhaps the most despised figure in the Elizabethan mentality: the Pope. Ricaredo states: "—Por la fe católica que mis cristianos padres me enseñaron, la cual si no está en la entereza que se requiere, por aquella juro que guarda el Pontífice romano, que es la que yo en mi corazón confieso, creo y tengo" (1: 270).[6] The text, then, openly and unreservedly posits the basic problem of religious dissidence,[7] subsequent persecution, fear of punishment, and the need for secrecy and hiding.

The phrase *católicos secretos* gives only a partial view of what the world of Clotaldo, his wife, and son Ricaredo was. History illuminates for us what the particular *vivencia* for all English Catholics was at the time. Cervantes only engages the aspect of secrecy, but it is precisely this secrecy that covers a larger and vaster area. Ricaredo and others maintain their secrecy precisely because the revelation of their religious practices would have resulted in serious punishment for them.

III

Henry VIII was responsible for a view that permeated attitudes toward Catholics during the reign of Elizabeth: Roman Catholicism was treason, since, in his opinion, allegiance to Rome represented allegiance to a foreign power (Plowden 46). Treason becomes one of the charges made with great frequency against both Catholic clergy and everyday practitioners of that faith.

The Oath of Supremacy laid out for the believer a clear road of conformity. Violation of this law meant punishment "by loss of benefice or office." For a first offense one could expect "the loss of benefice or property"; for a second, "premunire, loss of property and imprisonment at pleasure" (Morey 25); and for the third violation one could be tried for high treason. As Adrian Morey explains:

> The central act of worship of his faith, the Mass, was forbidden under penalty; recognition of the Pope as head of his religion was legal offence that might involve high treason; and access to the sacraments and religious instruction for his children were rarely possible. Although he was free to hold his religious convictions provided they were not given public expression, he was not permitted to worship as his convictions required. He had to conform to the new worship of the State Church in which he did not believe; attending its church services on Sundays and holydays and accepting the ministrations of its clergy. (Morey 42)

Plowden shows the dangers of sympathy with the Pope, that is, anyone who through writing and other verbal means "maintained and defended the spiritual or ecclesiastic jurisdiction of any foreign prince or prelate (i.e., the Pope) could lose all his goods and chattels for a first offense, lose all his property and go to prison for life for a second offense, and suffer the penalties of high treason for the third offense" (50). Serious penalties were meted out to anyone who spoke ill of the prescribed Prayer Book or heard or caused a clergyman to use a service other than the canonically accepted one (Plowden 50).

Chapter Two

Recusancy had its penalties. Attendance at the state rite was obligatory. Nonattendance could bring a summons to appear before a duly vested authority. It was common for offenders to ignore such a summons, yet doing so would leave one open to excommunication. Recusants could live with such excommunication, since some of the penalties were difficult to carry out (Morey 50).

Around the year 1571, the Treasons Act stipulated that to suggest or write that Elizabeth did not lawfully reign or to describe her as a "heretic, schismatic, tyrant, infidel or usurper" (Morey 60) was considered high treason. A second act prohibited the introduction of more formal Catholic action, such as bulls or articles of devotion, and "made it treason to reconcile anyone to the see of Rome or to receive such absolution" (Morey 60). One can understand why Ricaredo would conceal his trip to Rome in which he seeks absolution. A third act related to exiles, with similar penalties provided. The presence of Catholic recusants tended to intensify the belief of the faithful and in some cases convinced persons to remain Catholics who were wavering on whether they wished to remain faithful or become practicing Anglicans. All of this became a question of importance for governmental authorities. Morey says:

> In future, anyone claiming to have authority to absolve or withdraw any subjects from their natural obedience, or to withdraw them with that intent from the official religion to Catholicism, together with any persons so reconciled, were guilty of treason; anyone aiding or concealing this offense was guilty of misprision of treason. The penalty for celebrating Mass became a year's imprisonment and a fine of 200 marks; attendance at Mass incurred a year's imprisonment and a fine of 100 marks. Neale has argued that the 1581 Act "drew a statesmanlike distinction between being and becoming a Catholic": the Act did not plainly define conversion as an act of treason; it was conversion with intent to withdraw a subject from his allegiance that was treasonable, thus making the approach political and secular. (64–65)

Another interesting feature of the economic penalties that were levied on Catholics was the resulting increase in revenue that helped support various other political ventures. "In addition to the regular fines recusants were asked occasionally to pay extra-taxation: for example in 1580, 1584, 1585 and 1598 there were levies for the supply of light horsemen for the wars in Ireland and the Netherlands" (Morey 69).

In this negative, anti-Catholic atmosphere, a bill was presented to the House of Commons in 1593 that provided penalties for refusal to attend church and included

> seizure of all goods and the profits of two-thirds of a recusant's estate; no recusant would be permitted to lease, rent or sell land; recusant wives were henceforth to lose their dowers; the penalty for marriage to a recusant heiress was to be forfeiture of two-thirds of her inheritance; Catholics were to be excluded from all offices and the learned professions; anyone keeping a recusant guest or servant in his house was to pay a fine of £10 a month; and children were now to be removed from recusant parents at the age of 7 years and educated as Protestants. Thus, in the words of Neale, Catholics were to be treated as "an alien pest in society, immobilized, rendered impotent by virtual expropriation . . . and eradicated in a single generation." (Morey 70)

Morey continues:

> Queen Elizabeth has won great praise for her moderation in religious matters, yet it seems unlikely that, as Neale has suggested, she was unaware of this proposed Bill. (70)

The bill was not passed but another less stringent one was. The original bill was judged dangerous because it could also have applied to Protestants.

Further steps to control Catholics and their involvement around the country included the Five Mile Act of 1593:

> Recusants must now remain within five miles of their homes or forfeit goods and income from land; They must report to the minister and the parish constable, and their names were to be kept in a parish register and certified to the justices of the peace; Those who lacked a property qualification sufficient to enable them to pay the fines now became liable to banishment; and one clause that had condemned to death arrested persons suspected of being Jesuits, or secular priests who refused to admit their priesthood, was scaled down to imprisonment without trial. (Morey 70–71)

Chapter Two

Edward I. Watkin says regarding the Gunpowder Plot and Robert Cecil's legislation against Catholics:

> Heavy fines were enacted for recusants who did not receive Communion once a year in their parish church. The treason of reconciling a convert, or being reconciled, could now be committed abroad. Householders were made responsible for the recusancy of a guest or servant. Catholics were forbidden to reside within ten miles of London and a prohibition on journeying more than five miles from home, just imposed in 1593, was renewed. (63–64)

As early as 1561 efforts to limit the freedom of circulation of Catholics are recorded:

> Although the government attitude during the early years was relatively mild it maintained a steady pressure in religious matters. A list prepared for the Privy Council in 1561 included a number of prominent Catholics who were in prison, and others at liberty were restricted to particular districts to isolate them from places where they might have influence. Catholics who attempted to hear Mass in the London embassies were arrested, and periodic raids were made on houses where Mass was likely to be celebrated. (Morey 46)

There were of course severe attacks on priests (see Plowden 218–19, for a list and number of priests killed from 1581 to the 1590s). In 1585 an act was passed against "'Jesuits, seminary priests, and such like other disobedient persons'" (Watkin 33). The most notable example of antipriest penalties was that of Edmund Campion, to whom considerable torture was administered. He was subjected to a mock trial that ultimately ended in his death.[8] But examples like that of Campion served to help create a myth of Catholic martyrology that went a long way in reinforcing Catholic opposition to Protestants. As Watkin says: "Right-handed action, the seminaries, the composition and publication of Catholic literature, patient and valiant endurance of fine, imprisonment and the martyr's death, had ensured the survival of the Catholic religion in England" (60–61).

There were several other features in anti-Catholic persecution that should be duly noted. Any Catholic who undertook litigation ran the risk of being charged with treason. Catholic doctors ran particular risks if their patients did not recover (Morey 138). Thomas Plumtree, a chaplain to Northern insurgents, was put to death in 1570. John Story, having denied royal supremacy, was also killed in 1571 (Watkin 32). Priests who were ordained overseas since 1559 were given forty days to leave the area: "Those who remain and do not take the Oath of Supremacy within three days are guilty of treason, all who give them shelter or maintenance of felony, then a capital offense" (Watkin 33). Watkin notes that the recusant was "condemned to pay £20 every lunar month or forfeit two-thirds of his possessions" (59–60). According to Brian Magee, a Recusant cited by Watkin, "In the case of the vast majority 'there is ample evidence that the estates of recusants were universally undervalued'" (60). Land worth £2,000 was valued at £50. Watkin succinctly describes the difficulty of Catholics:

> Many Catholics spent years in prison. The heaviest burden was the insecurity. The penal code left Catholics without the right to property, were the fines duly enacted, to liberty, or even, since many had been reconciled and supported the missionaries and accepted their ministrations, the right to live. Whatever they might possess, property, freedom, even life, lay at the mercy of the Government. Under such conditions the endeavour to maintain the old religion must often have seemed a losing battle. Such in fact it proved to be, though never total defeat. (60)

In all fairness, it must be understood that the custom of undervaluation was by no means limited to recusants. And of course minimizing the value of one's property had tax advantages. But when the action was applied to recusants, it carried the suggestion of penalty, just as in Spain laws and edicts were promulgated against its minorities in much the same manner.

The polemic between Catholics and Protestants embraced, as we see, more than strictly religious issues. It dealt with political and social issues as well. Perhaps Kenneth L. Campbell put it best when he focused upon the issue of tolerance. He repeated the arguments expressed in a 1604 pamphlet by John Colleton:

> Catholics should not be punished for believing in the religion they view as the only means of saving their souls

Chapter Two

> eternally. [John] Colleton accepted minority status of Catholics and did not ask for special privileges. He merely wanted to see the penal laws reversed and the practice of the Catholic religion allowed in private houses. Furthermore, if James [I] reversed the penal laws Catholics would demonstrate more loyalty than anyone else because of their gratefulness; not to mention the fact that James would benefit in his foreign policy as well. (40–41)

While compromise and understanding may have been the desired end to this problem, the reality was different, and Cervantes's text, with its references to secrecy, highlights the penalizing attitude of the government toward Catholics.

Cervantes's awareness of the historical reality of Catholics and Protestants in England is revealed in his use of the Scottish presence; in this text it is relegated to the character of Clisterna. In two instances we see that Clisterna is also a secret Catholic (245, 270). Mary Stuart did have some support in her quest for the throne. Those that supported her did not forget or forgive her execution easily. Clisterna, as a character, intensifies the Catholic/Protestant conflict.

In the early years of her reign, Elizabeth put no Catholics to death, which could be interpreted as a tolerant attitude toward them.[9] The Pope's Bull of Excommunication was a defensive response by the Roman See to Elizabeth's Act of Supremacy. The Pope's bull, however, as Morey states, "came after ten years of conciliatory overtures from Rome" (56). Contact with English Catholics by Spaniards is easily documented (see Johnson, "'La española inglesa'" 390 ff.; see also Morey, who notes that in 1589 English and Irish students in Valladolid were befriended by Philip II [111]). As Morey also notes, "English merchants of the fraternity St. George had presented their house and chapel at San Lucar de Barrameda as a hospice for priests and students travelling to and fro [sic] England" (112). He further notes that in 1603, 32 members of the Spanish Court, including the Duke of Medina Sidonia, were extremely generous to English students and helped support them in colleges (112). The city of Seville, which occupies a prominent place in the dénouement of "La española inglesa," became well acquainted with English students and was generous toward them (Morey 112).

Católicos secretos

In response to a measure presented to the lower house, Robert Atkinson argued against some of the penalties and discrimination against Catholics and

> arguing that the maintenance of papal jurisdiction had never been considered to be treasonable, and that Englishmen should note the example of Germany "where after long contention and so great destruction of their country, at last they are come to this point that the Papist and Protestant can now talk quietly together . . . in this bill though a man intended to live under a law and keep his conscience to himself, yet by the oath we will grope him and see what lieth secretly in his breast." In the House of Lords Viscount Montague claimed that the law was unnecessary: "The Catholics of this realm disturb not, nor hinder the public affairs of this realm, neither spiritual nor temporal." (Morey 47)

Both the Appellants (a group of priests who appealed to Rome when George Blackwell was appointed as archpriest [Holmes 186]) and Persons, who under normal circumstances were in disagreement, believed that toleration and the revoking of all anti-Catholic laws would solve problems of hostility between the Catholic and Protestant camps. Persons also believed that the Catholics should be allowed their own "churches, bishops and colleges in England" (Holmes 214). However, as Holmes perceptively notes, such a resolution created certain political consequences:

> But the Queen, he [Persons] said, could not make such concessions, since it would arouse too much opposition among Protestants in England. Nevertheless, despite all this, he concluded that the Jesuits and the Archpriest [Blackwell] "greatly desire that the Catholics should gain liberty of conscience." (214)

Noting that heretics in France enjoyed liberty of conscience, Persons felt that Catholics in England and Ireland should have the same freedom. As Holmes puts it:

> All laws against Catholics in England ought to be repealed. No Catholic should be accused of treason on account of his religion, or forced to go to Protestant churches. Catholics should be allowed one church in each county, or, if this was impossible, freedom to celebrate mass in their homes. (214)

Chapter Two

He continues: "Exiles ought to be allowed to return, and free passage of students and missionaries to and from the seminaries should be permitted" (214). He concludes by saying that these suggestions did not come about in 1598. However, when further peace discussions took place in 1600, Persons broached the question of toleration and felt that it should be brought up within those discussions (Holmes 214). Persons wished to oppose some of Charles Paget's proposals, which reappeared in the policies of the Appellants, i.e., "that toleration for Catholics might be given in return for the expulsion of Jesuits; but, on the other hand, he seemed genuinely interested in the hope of freedom of religion which the peace negotiations seemed to hold" (Holmes 213).

For some, James I might have represented a change in policy, and there is reason to think that when "La española inglesa" was written, Cervantes may have been engaging in some wishful thinking regarding the fate of English Catholics (that is, if they are the ones he was really thinking about), although James is never referred to in the tale.[10]

Persons envisioned an ideal society and situation in which all parties managed to get along. However, it was just a dream in his mind, much as Cervantes himself must have dreamed about an ideal society of his own in which all members, majority and minorities, lived together in peace and tranquillity:

> In the English Catholic literary tradition, statements of loyalty to the Queen had, since 1580, been accompanied by the request for toleration, and this tradition continued in the works of Persons and his party in the last years of Elizabeth's reign. At the end of *A temperate ward-word* Persons expressed the hope that the Queen and her council would, like Henry IV of France, be converted to Catholicism. But, if this was impossible, he expressed the wish that Catholics might "have the same liberty and favour in England for their consciences as Protestants have in France and in other states of the Empire at this day under Catholic kings and emperors." (Holmes 211–12)

In his careful analysis of the economic background of "La española inglesa," Johnson touches lightly on a problem that applies eminently to Golden Age studies. Focusing on the dilemma of the English Catholics, he notes, "In fact, their situa-

Católicos secretos

tion bears a striking resemblance to that of the *conversos* in Cervantes's own society, of whom Isabela and her family are a fictional representation" ("'La española inglesa'" 386). Johnson further states that "The text affirms the superiority of a capitalistic economic system in the hands of the probably New Christian (but for all that splendidly Catholic) bourgeoisie over a feudal economy in the hands of the aristocracy, as presented by official rhetoric" (415).

My contention is that Cervantes in this story and on this point is working on two levels, as he does in "La gitanilla." The initial text addresses the quandary of English Catholics, but there is a subtext that in fact deals with the dilemma of Jews and *conversos*. Of the two dilemmas it would seem reasonable to assume that the dilemma of Jews and *conversos* represented for Cervantes and his readership a problem of greater immediacy than that of English Catholics. The characters, for all that is said of their "Britainicity," are Spanish characters functioning in false garb, much in the manner of pastoral characters in an arcadian landscape. The universality of the church would warrant curiosity and concern for the faithful living under the pressure of foreign and hostile regimes (e.g., in our own times, Cardinal Mindzenty and the Hungarian Communist regime; the fate of Maryknoll priests in Maoist China, etc.). But I hope to show that much of the behavior of Cervantes's characters in this tale could easily represent the peripeteia of *conversos* in Cervantes's own Spain. Therefore, I assert that the historical subtext, beneath its literary veil, does address the problems of Jews (and Moors) living as minority cultures in Spain, and under the same kinds of duress and life-threatening situations. The subtext, then, in this interesting interplay of "histories," would shape and be shaped by Cervantes's humanity toward this persecuted minority in much the same manner that he treats Gypsies in "La gitanilla." Elizabeth I could be replaced symbolically by Philip II and/or Philip III; Clotaldo and his family, by false Christians paying lip service to the demands of the dominant culture.[11] This perusal of history in England shows to what an extent the perils of being Catholic in England so greatly resembled those of being a *converso* in Spain.

A bishop makes a denunciation of Catholics in October of 1564: "some have Mass in their houses, 'come seldom or not

Chapter Two

at all to church, which never received the communion since the Queen's Majesty's reign . . . the communion was not ministered in the cathedral church since Easter'" (Morey 43).[12] Plowden refers to Edward Rishton, who says: "'At the same time . . . they had Mass said secretly in their own houses by those very priests who in church publicly celebrated the spurious liturgy, and sometimes by others who had not defiled themselves with heresy'" (48).

In the examples I see in English history (just as in the examples we know of in Spanish history), pretense and deception with respect to one's true faith were necessary for survival. Plowden states,

> One modern Catholic historian has summed up the position in words not so very different from Edward Rishton's. "The Queen's subjects may continue to be Catholics *so long as they pretend to be Protestants, and to live as Protestants and to use the new rites as though they are Protestants* [emphasis mine]. They do not need to believe anything of what they profess to believe."

She adds, "This may have been doubtful ethics, but it was sound political common sense" (51). She continues,

> There might be no question of giving Catholics their own places of worship, but Mass continued to be quite widely available for those who knew where to look for it: in quiet country houses where a sympathetic gentleman had given shelter to a deprived priest; in remote districts where, once the Queen's visitors had ridden away, priest and people continued to do just as they had always done; in London in the chapels of the French and Spanish embassies, where from time to time government agents arrived to take the names of those present. (52)

When Cervantes used the word *secret* he could not have been unaware of what that meant in his own society, where individuals forged documents of ancestry, and where *marranos* held secret rites in fear of death.[13] Watkin notes, "And there was the constant threat of pursuivants raiding a Catholic house and driving priests into the hiding places now being built to conceal them. Nor should one forget the fines and imprisonment often

Católicos secretos

for many years endured by large numbers of lay people, women as well as men" (50–51).

The principle of *malsinismo,* living life under the fear of an informer who watches the lives of others, was also applicable to the lives of Catholics in England: "In 1591 Elizabeth issued a proclamation against the Jesuits and seminary priests in which she ordered committees to be appointed in every parish to inquire into the church attendance of the parishioners" (Watkin 51). Campion, like Persons, had hoped that Catholics could be recognized as representatives of an earlier valued tradition, and as such, worthy of a peaceful life. Campion told the Lord Chief Justice in response to the usual question as to whether he had anything to say before being sentenced:

> "if our religion do make us traitors, we are worthy to be condemned; but otherwise are and have been as true subjects as ever the Queen had. In condemning us you condemn all your own ancestors—all the ancient priests, bishops and kings—all that was once the glory of England, the island of saints, and the most devoted child of the see of Peter."
> (Plowden 187)

This passage could have been written by a Spanish Jew or *converso* who, believing himself to be as Spanish as anyone else, had to recant, be reconciled to a religion not his own, be forced out of fear for his own life and that of his family to practice a religion in which he did not believe, yet never questioning his own Hispanicity. (For the question of religious equality, see Richard Shelley's petition to the Queen concerning the possible charge of treason for sheltering priests [Morey 66–67].)

It is not unreasonable to assume that the average cultivated Spanish reader of "La española inglesa" could see the first level (Britain and the English Catholics) as a pretext for self-criticism of Spain with the objective of promoting a religious norm that worked toward tolerance of faiths, a return in some way to a Medieval notion of *convivencia*.[14]

The characters in "La española inglesa" insist upon their Catholic faith and practice it secretly. On one level we have the Catholic faith and on top of it the stratum of false or feigned Anglicanism. It is easy to see how the conflict exists in the characters themselves, but Cervantes used Ricaredo to bring

Chapter Two

about a resolution that favored Catholicism. Moreover, his loyalty to the Roman church is reaffirmed when we are informed, "y Ricaredo salió a decir a sus padres como en ninguna manera no se casaría ni daría la mano a su esposa la escocesa sin haber primero ido a Roma a asegurar su conciencia" (271).[15] This, of course, is done keeping in mind the Pope's bull, *Regnans in Excelsis,* which excommunicated Elizabeth.

Protestant attitudes toward the Pope and Catholics were conditioned by the fact that the Pope favored the Armada enterprise. Morey reports the case of a Catholic doctor who did not sufficiently cure a patient and was accused "of being 'a notorious recusant and maintainer of popery'" (138). Concomitant with this awareness of papal authority was the presence of Rome as a religious symbol. Casalduero believes that Ricaredo's love confession is "una confesión de amor a la mayor gloria de Roma" (99). For the English at that time, Rome was considered another foreign power, and Ricaredo's pro-papal, pro-Roman stance is for me an acknowledgment that Spain is as much a political power as a religious force.

The subtext as a pro-*converso* allegation would contradict a total adherence by Cervantes to Catholic principles. Ricaredo and Isabel, not to mention Clotaldo and his wife as well as Clisterna, in their literary metamorphosis, are Spaniards, in spite of their pseudo-Britannic reconstruction, and the purpose is to express once again Cervantes's loyalty to his *patria* (see below, chapter 5, "*Apologia pro patria sua:* Cervantes's 'La señora Cornelia'").

The process of reading and writing that I am suggesting is very much like a practice by painters in the Renaissance: I refer to *pentimento*. In this process, an original painting is covered over by another one in such a way that after a period of time the outlines or the figures of the first painting begin to show through. Cervantes's handling of text and subtext is reminiscent of this process, and the original construction (i.e., the plight of *conversos* in a society that has tyrannized them) has resonance with the plight of English recusant Catholics.

IV

I have already outlined above the peculiarities of Elizabethan political and religious attitudes as they touched on the subject

Católicos secretos

for Philip II, the Armada, recusancy, the presence of Jesuits, and other issues of the times. On the one hand, in the Spanish view Elizabeth can be perceived as a severe, anti-Catholic queen and, as such, an "enemy of the people." On the other hand, in the tale she is a sympathetic, benevolent figure. This inconsistency must surely call for a "nonhistorical" explanation. Johnson is correct in stating that the queen of history and the queen of the tale are two different figures. Louis A. Montrose offers this insight into a similar use of the figure of Elizabeth in the works of Edmund Spenser:

> The dynamic principle here exemplified is that, as both the subject and his discourse are shaped by "the Queen"—and here I mean not the person of Elizabeth Tudor but rather the whole field of cultural meanings personified in her—so they also reshape the Queen by the very process of addressing and representing her. (303)

In his re-creation and refashioning of an historical figure that was "an enemy of the people," Cervantes stresses her benevolence, her caring for her subjects.[16] He has chosen to fashion her according to the multiple perspectives that his readers have. Greenblatt stresses that "Or rather, for the early sixteenth century, art does not pretend to autonomy; the written word is self-consciously embedded in specific communities, life situations, structures of power" (7). It is difficult for the modern reader not to see Elizabeth in terms of gender values. In his analysis, Montrose associates Elizabeth with a gender system in which male=superior and female=inferior (308). But in Cervantes's depiction of this historical figure, she is anything but inferior. Her strength lies in her equanimity and balance.

Cervantes's purpose, I believe, was to use one level, an historical and religious level, as a symbol and representation of the official persecution against *conversos* and Jews.[17] He creates an Elizabeth, a benevolent monarch, who treats her subjects with love and compassion; the guilty *camarera* gives Isabel poison and does so because she would be removing a Catholic from the earth. This explanation does not seem to find any sympathy with the fictional queen.

The historical figure of James I also must be viewed in this context. If Cervantes's purpose was to instill understanding and

Chapter Two

tolerance, the beginning of the reign of James I was a bad moment to depict Queen Elizabeth as evil. Johnson notes, "He [Cervantes] replaces a real, historical signifier of 1605—James I (peace and good will)—with another, from the period just ended—Elizabeth (antagonism of every kind). In addition, he relexicalizes a series of signs—dress, language, and the like—which had in fact lost much if not all of their power to indicate differences" ("'La española inglesa'" 398). He goes on to state further,

> The net result of this process is something like a return to the historical truth of 1605 and the possibilities of that moment, but expressed in the language of 1596. Furthermore, this text did not become public until 1613, when the signifiers and expectations of 1596 [the second attack on Cádiz] had again become valid. That is, the text subverts the attitudes and the expectations of the reader of 1613 and, as experience has shown, those of most succeeding generations of readers as well. (398)

Montrose observes an interesting phenomenon that can apply to the construction of this Elizabethan figure in Cervantes:

> Such a poem [as Spenser's pastoral poem] is not merely the *product* of a received ideology but is itself a distinctive *production* [Montrose's emphasis] of ideology, which, by representing the queen in a text, ineluctably reconstitutes the queen as a textual product. Thus, the poem may be said to reverse the official relationship of symbolic filiation: To metaphorize Elisa as the poet's offspring is an implicit response to the frequent metaphorizing of the queen as her subject's mother; it is a contestation of her status as cultural genetrix. (322)

Cervantes reconstructs Elizabeth as a competing monarch but in positive terms as part of an historical wish fulfillment on his part; he deconstructs history and refashions it along more desired lines.

This positive portrait should also warrant an investigation into the figure of Elizabeth's successor, James I. On his accession, he reduced fines for recusancy and did other things to warrant a cautious and nonaggressive attitude toward the English Catholics. As Campbell notes:

Católicos secretos

James drastically reduced the amount of recusancy fines leveled and seemed to favor a very lenient policy towards the Catholics. James's whole attitude and conduct, within his own court as well as in public affairs, showed that he could be a thoroughly reasonable man with a very practical outlook on religious differences. But Parliament interpreted this as either weakness or sympathy for Rome and refused to tolerate any move towards compromise with the papists. (39)

A 1603 pamphlet, the Edict of Nantes, and the tolerant policies of Henry IV were examples that James could follow. Another pamphlet in 1604 by Colleton (*A Supplication of the Kings most excellent Majestie, wherein, severall reasons of State and Religion are briefly touched*) also made useful suggestions to James (Campbell 40). Johnson quotes Icaza, who felt that the tale was composed in the period of rapprochement between England and Spain after James's succession to the throne (and this could account for Cervantes's positive depiction of Elizabeth I [" 'La española inglesa' " 388–89]). Furthermore, on James's accession to the throne, he freed many Roman Catholic priests who were in prison and he renewed his promises of toleration (Watkin 62).

Consequently, the portrayal of Elizabeth in the story is due more to the political exigencies of the historical moment, a moment further complicated by the intricacies of Cervantes's own psycho-social strivings uttered through his literature.

V

Johnson's analysis of "La española inglesa" hinges on the role of the siege of Cádiz of 1596. My view of this episode as an applicable background of the tale is different from his; I go beyond 1596. I establish a temporal matrix of Lepanto through the two sieges of Cádiz, the deaths of Elizabeth and Philip II, and the accession to the throne of James I. Within this temporal perspective I also emphasize the maritime components of that chronological span.

On April 18, 1587, a squadron of English ships under the command of Francis Drake entered the Bay of Cádiz and inflicted considerable damage on the Spanish fleet at anchor there.

Chapter Two

The appearance of Drake with his fleet did not instill any particular fear in the Spaniards, but the consequences of Cádiz 1 (I shall use this designation to refer to the siege of 1587 and Cádiz 2 to that of 1596) were to be far-reaching in terms of naval operations and warfare. What Drake's attack did was to bring to light weaknesses of the Spanish fleet in battle. It also inflicted on Spain a lesson that would greatly affect the future of Spanish naval power (see below). Quite aside from the fact that Drake obtained a substantial amount of booty, a not insignificant factor in naval operations of a privateering nature, the operation left Queen Elizabeth embarrassed. The blow to Spain's prestige could be seen as a cause for adverse political reactions on the part of Spain. This foray into the Spanish Bay of Cádiz gave one of the first indications that a principal ingredient of Spanish international power, her fleet, was rotting away with incompetence and outdated weaponry. Concerning Drake's expedition, Garrett Mattingly says:

> There the heavier English ships were engaged first with Don Pedro de Acuña's galleys in a fight the outcome of which can never have been very doubtful to either side. It is tempting to talk of the beginning of a new era of naval warfare in Cadiz Bay, of the unexpected triumph of the Atlantic over the Mediterranean, and the end of the two-thousand-year rule of seas by the galley. (98)

Cádiz 1 gave the first intimations of future disaster.

In June of 1596 a new expedition under the command of the Earl of Essex and Admiral Howard entered the Bay of Cádiz, destroyed and sacked the city, and devastated the Spanish ships anchored in the harbor. According to Rafael Altamira, this happening "Tal fue, por entonces, el último episodio de la guerra con Inglaterra" (3: 105). The Duke of Medina Sidonia's comportment in this episode has left a cloud over his head. Johnson is particularly severe in imputing more than just incompetence on his part (see "'La española inglesa'" 382 ff.). In his economic-historical approach, Johnson focuses on the fact that the vessels in Cádiz harbor were filled with goods destined for the New World (380). He suggests that after the destruction of the fleet at Cádiz, Seville achieved greater importance as an economic center, so that the destruction wrought by England in

Católicos secretos

Cádiz 2 not only destroyed an important part of the Spanish fleet but led to the taking of a considerable amount of booty from both the city and the ships. For the second time England damaged the "myth" of Spanish maritime invincibility and showed decisively that the English ships could move quickly and take advantage of the older Spanish fleet. This expedition repeated the consequences of the first Cádiz defeat, another sign of the decline of Spanish power and an omen of the debacle of the Armada.

The Armada enterprise, like a number of other events in Spanish Golden Age involvements from Charles V to Philip II, was endowed with religious, crusading overtones. Mattingly reports a story that shows this attitude. The Pope sent a special emissary to Lisbon to ascertain some facts in order to be able to support Philip II's enterprise:

> Just a few days before the ceremony of the standard this observer had reported to Cardinal Montalto an illuminating conversation. He was talking privately, he said, to one of the highest and most experienced officers of the Spanish fleet (can it have been Juan Martínez de Recalde?) and found the courage to ask him bluntly: "And if you meet the English Armada in the Channel, do you expect to win the battle?" "Of course," replied the Spaniard. "How can you be sure?" "It's very simple. It is well known that we fight in God's cause. So, when we meet the English, God will surely arrange matters so that we can grapple and board them, either by sending some strange freak of weather or, more likely just by depriving the English of their wits. If we can come to close quarters, Spanish valour and Spanish steel (and the great masses of soldiers we shall have on board) will make a victory certain. But unless God helps us by a miracle the English, who have faster and handier ships than ours, and many more long-range guns, and who know their advantage just as well as we do, will never close with us at all, but stand aloof and knock us to pieces with their culverins, without our being able to do them any serious hurt. So," concluded the captain, and one fancies with a grim smile, "we are sailing against England in the confident hope of a miracle." (202–03)

It is ironic that after the fall of the Armada there was a similar position taken by Protestants:

Chapter Two

> The Protestants of France and the Netherlands, Germany and Scandinavia saw with relief that God was in truth, as they had always supposed, on their side. The Catholics of France and Italy and Germany saw with almost equal relief that Spain was not, after all, God's chosen champion. From that time forward, though Spain's preponderance was to last for more than another generation, the peak of her prestige had passed. (Mattingly 356)

Philip II envisioned a vast undertaking for which his fleet and supplies were unprepared. Concerning the actual battle, Mattingly says,

> There was enough cause for uncertainty. Fleets like these were a new thing in the world. Nobody had ever seen two such in combat. Nobody knew what the new weapons would do, or what tactics would make them most effective. This was the beginning of a new era in naval warfare, of the long day in which the ship-of-the-line, wooden-walled, sail-driven and armed with smooth-bore cannon, was to be queen of battles; a day for which the armour-plated, steam powered battleship with rifled cannon merely marked the evening, so that antiquarians will probably lump the two together when they have thought of a name for the period which, until just now, we have called "modern." In the beginning there was no name for the ship-of-the-line, and no idea how to use it. That morning off the Eddystone nobody in either fleet knew how to fight a "modern" battle. Nobody in the world knew how. (252–53)

The myth of Spanish power proved to be greater than its reality, and this failure meant a tremendous blow to Spanish power, prestige, and image in the political and economic affairs of Europe and the New World.[18] By the end of the fiasco there were no longer the resources left to pick up the pieces and attempt another operation to restore Spain's lost honor. This, in spite of the fact that Philip had broached the question of the possibility of a second Armada in 1596–97, no doubt still with a lingering religious notion in his mind.

One must examine this succession of events in their totality to see what effects it had on Cervantes. For him, the greatest event of his life was his participation in the Battle of Lepanto. This battle against the Turks meant that his culture was powerful and religiously, certifiably just. Yet, as time went on, the greatness of Spain, just as powerful as at Lepanto, evanesced under the incompetence and misjudgments of Philip II, his advisors and admirals. The reality of a Spain now militarily and navally crippled must have affected Cervantes, who had the experience of defending its colors against the Turks.

Given the particular historical atmosphere and background of "La española inglesa," it is not accidental, in my view, that a portion of the plot deals with the sea and other maritime data. The politics of the era hinged greatly on the factor of sea power and can be read in phrases such as "cuando suba o baje el turco." Within the maritime view Cervantes manages to include Turks, without whom his treatment of the maritime myth would have been woefully incomplete. Yet, given the hypotheses of Cervantes's wish for toleration of Spain's own minorities *(conversos, cristianos nuevos,* Gypsies, and others) that I have advanced, how interesting it is that the Turks appear less hostile and antagonistic than might have been warranted in that time. After the introduction of the motif of the "galeras turquescas," Ricaredo as the new captain of the expedition gives freedom to the Turks, a daring move, and an action similar to the greater action of giving freedom to Catholics. In a later episode, as if to show that toleration and generosity of spirit can be had in "minority" peoples, Ricaredo is recognized by one of the Turks that he freed, who then saves Ricaredo. The symbolism of such an ironic turn should not be understressed. Such phrases implicitly acknowledged Spain's sea power, which was very much a part of the popular mythology of the time, just as the phrase "los tercios españoles" alluded to Spanish troops stationed in different parts of the globe. The presence of *ars maritima* in this story catered to the "thirst" of the public for matters that dealt with seafaring, pirates, privateers, and voyages to the New World. I believe that the earlier maritime history from Lepanto to the Armada serves as a critical political, economic, and social background to the tale, because it must have been tempting for Cervantes to include this information in his story, a temptation moreover to which he succumbed. Plowden notes that Spanish coasters with Spanish bullion arrived at Plymouth and were seized by Elizabeth I (81). Such activities whether done independently by pirates or privateers (often supported

Chapter Two

and encouraged by Elizabeth) were well known and were the cause of further aggravation of relations between Spain and England. Seizures such as the one at Plymouth helped fill the English coffers (as did the forays against Spain both times in Cádiz).

What is particularly impressive in the maritime allusions and creations is the accuracy in dealing with *materia maritima*. An example will suffice:

> al cabo de los cuales [meses] vine a Génova, donde no hallé otro pasaje sino en dos falugas que fletamos yo y otros dos principales españoles, la una para que fuese delante descubriendo y la otra donde nosotros fuésemos. Con esta seguridad nos embarcamos, navegando tierra a tierra con intención de no engolfarnos; pero llegando a un paraje que llaman las Tres Marías, que es en la costa de Francia, yendo nuestra primera faluga descubriendo, a deshora salieron de una cala dos galeotas turquescas, y tomándonos la una la mar y la otra la tierra, cuando íbamos a embestir en ella, nos cortaron el camino y nos cautivaron. (1: 280–81)

This description reveals a sure knowledge of ships, routes, geography and other marine data. Cervantes had participated in the Battle of Lepanto; he had traveled by sea to Italy and journeyed around the Mediterranean basin and North Africa. The text says: "Seis dias navegaron los dos navíos, con próspero viento, siguiendo la derrota de las islas Terceras, paraje donde nunca faltan o naves portuguesas de las Indias orientales o algunas derrotadas de las occidentales" (1: 252). Cervantes's descriptions of Ricaredo's voyages are strong and accurate. Encounters with Portuguese ships, such as occur in the text, must have called to mind famous encounters like the one in 1592: "In 1592 Fortune smiled again. In the Azores Cumberland's ships, in the company of others, captured the great Portuguese carrack the *Madre de Dios,* laden with a huge cargo of jewels, spices, silks and other precious goods" (Andrews 73). They also contain what is important for me: the myth of freedom embodied in the travel on the infinite seas. This concept was as meaningful for the Spanish seventeenth-century reader as it was for the Greek listening public and its tales of the travels of Ulysses: "Preguntóles Ricaredo en español que

Católicos secretos

qué navío era aquel. Respondiéronle que era una nave que venía de la India de Portugal, cargada de especería, y con tantas perlas y diamantes, que valía más de un millón de oro" (1: 254). Such allusions had special meaning for a nation that traded with the other countries of Europe. There are further links between the text and history on the question of privateering and in general on the reality and myth of the maritime life:

> The seaman's life aboard a privateer was nasty, brutish and short. His diet at the beginning of a voyage might consist of bread or biscuit, oatmeal or peasemeal, salted beef or pork, fish, butter, cheese and beer, but even then gave no defence against scurvy, that "plague of the sea and the spoil of mariners." In any case before long the food would go bad and the beer sour. Dysentery—the "bloody flux"—was inevitable in the filthy conditions which prevailed, and especially common when the ships reached warmer climates or captured cargoes of wine. And in spite of the readiness of privateers to rob other vessels of provisions, the crews sometimes simply starved to death, as did most of the men in John Chidley's *Robin*. In these respects the overcrowded and undisciplined crew of a privateer was likely to suffer more than that of a royal ship. But since the causes of disease were not understood, *the freedom associated with privateer service acted only as an attraction to sailors* [emphasis mine]. (Andrews 40)

There is an echo of this in Cervantes's text: "y que con tormenta había arribado a aquella parte, toda destruida y sin artillería, por haberla echado a la mar la gente, enferma y casi muerta de sed y de hambre" (1: 254). In an effort not to antagonize his crew, Ricaredo consults them on action to be taken: "No le parecieron mal a Ricaredo las razones del español, y llamando a consejo los de su navío, les preguntó cómo haría para enviar todos los cristianos a España sin ponerse a peligro de algún siniestro suceso, si el ser tantos les daba ánimo para levantarse" (1: 255). Andrews notes: "Drunkenness and disorder aboard ship became common, uncontrolled violence and lawlessness at sea developed by the end of the war into a general menace to commerce, and attempts to impose discipline met with mutiny" (41). "La India de Portugal" existed as a mythical concept of an exotic yet materially rich nature just as "el Nuevo

65

Chapter Two

Mundo" symbolized the untold riches of Mexico and Peru. Andrews informs us that

> In 1584 Philip of Spain confirmed the privileges of the English merchants in Portugal and it was not until 1589 that they were finally expelled from Lisbon. But the whole situation was changed by the Spanish confiscations of 1585. English privateers now regarded Portuguese shipping anywhere as fair game. (206)

Andrews also reports that about 1589–91 approximately 1,000 Spanish and Portuguese ships were captured by the English during the course of the war (224). Moreover, "It was reported in December 1597 that 'the merchants of Seville and Portugal who used to venture to the Indies are broken by losses of goods and ships since the wars'" (Andrews 226). Therefore, these allusions dealing with Portuguese ships were not mere *inventio*. They recalled for the wealthy class and the class of merchant seamen and soldiers the military enterprises in which many had participated. Cervantes re-created the adventures narrated in chronicles and other media to illustrate one of his most cherished themes—the myth of the sea.

There is a description of Isabel that I believe is an indirect acknowledgment of the history and economics of the time:

> Con esto se consolaron, y acordaron que Isabela no fuese vestida humildemente, como prisionera, sino como esposa, pues ya lo era de tan principal esposo como su hijo. Resueltos en esto, otro día vistieron a Isabela a la española, con una saya entera de raso verde acuchillada y forrada en rica tela de oro, tomadas las cuchilladas con unas eses de perlas, y toda ella bordada de riquísimas perlas; collar y cintura de diamantes, y con abanico a modo de las señoras damas españolas; sus mismos cabellos, que eran muchos, rubios y largos, entretejidos y sembrados de diamantes y perlas, le servían de tocado. (1: 248)[19]

With such a stress on clothes, one can better understand and agree with Johnson, who cogently posits the idea that all textiles belonged to foreign merchant capitalists, especially the English and Dutch.[20]

Johnson presents perhaps the strongest case for an economic reading of the story as *another* backdrop to its understanding.

Católicos secretos

While I do not embrace his analysis completely, I accept the place of an economic reading of this tale. It is my belief that the strongest case to be made in an extratextual analysis is the religious and historical one, and I have preferred this more than an economic one. Johnson's reading, however, is the best example of an economic analysis.

It cannot be forgotten that the parents of Isabel return to Seville. Johnson points out that there was a rivalry between Seville and Cádiz, and the Duke of Medina Sidonia was allied with Sevillian merchant interests. The siege of 1596 virtually, if however temporarily, destroyed Cádiz as an emerging center of commerce (Johnson, "'La española inglesa'" 384). Johnson further insists that "Cervantes's membership in the business and financial community, particularly in the locations crucial to the gestation of *La española inglesa*, is amply documented" (413).[21]

There is yet another datum that I wish to discuss, and that deals with the name of the character Ricaredo and an analogous person from Visigothic history: Recaredo, king of the Visigoths from 586 to 601 and an able military strategist (Thompson 111).[22] Part of the Recaredo's reign involves the wars and polemics between Catholics and Arians (fourth-century heretics) and the theological break between them. Recaredo converted to Catholicism and many followed him.[23] Chronicles depict him in the following way:

> Este rey Recaredo fue muy alongado de las costumbres de su padre [Leovigildo], et non era marauilla ca ell era ensennado de sant Leandro arçobispo de Seuilla quel ennennara a creer en la fe de Nostro Sennor Dios, et por ende la amaua ell et la tenie muy bien; e quanto el padre fue muy cruel a los de la fe de Cristo et muy guerrero, tanto fue este Recaredo piadoso et de paz contra todos en amar los et querer los bien.
> ... E luego que començo a regnar enuio por sant Leandro e sant Ffulgencio e por Mausona, los arçobispos e por todos los otros que fueran desterrados; e torno todos los pueblos a la fe de Ihesu Cristo et tiro los dell yerro en que estauan.[24]

The period of his reign is looked upon as a victory of "the true faith" over a similar, but theologically different group—Arians—and politically as a time of increased dominance of the Visigothic reign over Hispano-Romans. I do not wish to

Chapter Two

oversimplify what is a complicated religious and political process. My thesis is that Cervantes wrote "La española inglesa" using a set of masquerading symbols: Roman Catholics versus English Protestants for *conversos* versus traditional Catholics in seventeenth-century Spain. Recaredo becomes then a symbol of religious strife, of religious dedication, of personal valor (just as we see the heroics of Ricaredo in the text). During Recaredo's reign there were many contacts with Jews. He oversaw forced conversion of Jews, and there were laws that penalized Jews in the traffic of Christian slaves. However, the Fourth Council of Toledo in 633, during the reign of King Sisebuto, inveighed against those churchmen who protected Jews from persecution (see Thompson 133). In effect, the reigns of Leovigildo (Recaredo's father), Recaredo, and Sisebuto were characterized by a persecution of Jews and other minorities. I do not think that my use of the name Recaredo/Ricaredo is particularly injurious to my thesis in spite of the fact that Recaredo indulged in anti-Semitic acts. What is important is the resonance in the popular and even erudite mind that the name Recaredo had. Is it possible that Cervantes and his readership could neglect to see some of the overtones that the name Ricaredo/Recaredo held? This is, for me, yet another example of the historical contagion of the Cervantine text.

In conclusion, in "La española inglesa," Cervantes used a multiple level approach to present his ideas. The first level is the conflict of *católicos secretos* in a hostile England. This first level is a text superimposed on a more basic, truly indigenous Spanish conflict: the presence and treatment of Spain's own minorities—Jews, Moors, *conversos*. The initial level of action utilizes a mythical motif (the myth of the sea) as symbolized in the maritime experiences and maritime world to reinforce the play between text and subtext.

Using all the historical, economic, religious, and literary threads, I interpret once again a critical attitude on the part of Cervantes toward his own historical reality: it is the shaken pride of someone who always clung proudly to the symbol of Lepanto and watched the greatness and power of Spain dwindle and wane until the end of the reign of Philip II and the beginning of that of Philip III. The once great moment has disappeared, and Cervantes must live with the subtext of *desengaño* beneath the main foot of glory.

Chapter Three

"El licenciado Vidriera,"
or "La historia de un fracaso"

"El licenciado Vidriera" represents for me one of the best examples of history and literature blended into one unit. There exists an historical and social backdrop to this story that brings coherency to the tale, and at the same time we see Cervantes's concern with the literary intertextuality and some features of narrativity.[1]

This novel uses for its basic focus a university career in law. The character receives a licentiate of law degree from Salamanca, which confers upon him a certain amount of prestige. Since Cervantes is a native of Alcalá de Henares, it might seem a bit strange that he chose Salamanca for his character rather than Alcalá. Salamanca and Alcalá (along with Valladolid) were the three major Spanish universities of the time. Quite apart from any civic loyalty Cervantes may have felt to Alcalá, Salamanca came to symbolize the true student's life and was a symbol in Spain of university affairs (Defourneaux 165). It is well known that Alcalá in the sixteenth century was famous for its curriculum in theology, whereas law formed one of the most prestigious curricula and careers at Salamanca (Jiménez 162). It was not until the seventeenth century that law was brought into the curriculum at Alcalá, contrary to the intentions of Cardinal Cisneros, its founder (Jiménez 166). At the same time it must be noted that Salamanca was viewed as the more liberal and more democratic institution, while Alcalá was strongly influenced by foreign elements (García Mercadal 40). Henry Kamen (76) observes that in the 1550s there was a visible decadence of liberal traditions at Alcalá. This not only signified a breakdown of traditions of openness in Alcalá but also marked the end of an important and more tolerant period of culture in Spain.

Chapter Three

Tomás Rueda's choice of a career in law also provokes a number of considerations. In his excellent study of law and litigation in Castile during the period 1500–1700, Richard Kagan notes (*Law* 136) that the great economic expansion that occurred in that period, as well as the growth of population, brought with it conditions and situations that created a need for lawyers to handle the numerous problems that arose from this expansion and growth. The idea of friends litigating against friends was incompatible with a religious picture of people getting along and resolving their difficulties amicably (Kagan, *Law* 20). But the departure from more conventional and ideal ways of settling disputes only serves to accentuate the fact that Spain had left behind it a society based upon traditional moral values. These values were now replaced, if we are to believe Kagan's argument, by the value system of a diverse society.

This proliferation of lawyers to handle the increased needs for litigation, and the possible moral significance of such an increase, did not go unnoticed: "Content to mediate conflict, rather than work to establish a truly just and Christian world, lawyers were moral anarchy personified and said to be one of the major reasons why Castile had lost God's grace" (Kagan, *Law* 73). In 1624, Fray Angel Manrique saw the situation as detrimental to the public weal: " 'the abundance of licentiates who ignore necessary jobs is not good for the Republic' " (cited by Kagan, *Stud.* 234). The expansion must have been significant for Manrique, but while Kagan acknowledges the increase in *bachilleres* (of law), he also states that the number of advanced degrees being granted was not large, thus making Licenciado Vidriera a special case (*Law* 142).

The social class of *labradores,* peasants, and other country people in itself posed a problem of an educational nature. Educational access was more open for the children of urban areas than for those from rural ones. Literacy was distributed in direct proportion to population density (with *rus* playing second to *urbs*). Consequently, even if poor children received an education their parents had lacked, they had to compete later with those who came from a tradition of literacy rather than illiteracy (Kagan, *Stud.* 180–81). In the final phase of the problem, employment possibilities were far greater for the children of the well-to-do than for the children of poor country farmers.

"El licenciado Vidriera"

The touchstone of education was Latin and study of the classics. In terms of education and social mobility, this tended to separate the two dominant classes (Kagan, *Stud.* 50, 59). Early in the establishment of *colegios mayores* some accommodations were made to provide for the education of promising, poor students (Domínguez Ortiz, *Golden Age* 233). There was another opportunity for study open to aspiring poor or less advantaged scholars: as servants of wealthy or well-to-do students (Tomás Rodaja gets his education thanks to the social station of the two Málaga youths he serves).

That Rodaja is from a poor rural family should not be overlooked for its signficance in the background of the story. Such graduates were viewed with alarm by some in the educated classes. Institutionally and privately, steps were taken to hamper or hinder the educational progress of the poor and those who practiced manual arts, which encouraged the creation of an aristocratic and noble elite. (On this subject see Creel, *Don Quijote, Symbol*). Some viewed the proximity of a university as a distraction for the peasant class (Kagan, *Stud.* 44–45). This reservation is best seen in one of the complaints registered in the Junta de Reformación (1621):

> it would also help to reform some grammar schools newly founded in villages and small places, because with the opportunity of having them so near, the peasants (*labradores*) divert their sons from the jobs and occupations in which they were born and raised, and put them to study from which they benefit little . . . (Kagan, *Stud.* 44–45)

Kagan also states:

> A century before, increases in the number of schoolboys were held partly responsible for the decline of Spain, since educated youths were accused of abandoning fields and work shops to the detriment of the national economy. (*Stud.* 46)[2]

In the sixteenth century both Alcalá and Salamanca were open theoretically to all Christians; but as the liberal and democratic quality of these institutions weakened, the universities became largely the meeting place of the rich and noble. In time the *letrados,* because the law was a very practical field of study

Chapter Three

that led to positions and jobs, came to constitute a separate social class (Maravall passim). Because of their numbers and the growing influence that was attached to the *letrados,* especially if they were at the sources of power, the *letrado* class could not but be viewed as a threat to established aristocratic families (see Maravall 384–85, 388–89).

Consequently, Tomás Rodaja's experience—i.e., his education and the degrees he takes—corresponds to a particular social and educational situation common to Spain and to his class. Given the social difficulties under which Rodaja has obviously labored, his success is presented by Cervantes as an admirable accomplishment, as I am sure that the average literate reader of his time sensed in reading the story.

Strictly in terms of structure, I see the *novela* as existing as a triptych. The two flanking sides are formed by the early career of Rodaja as a student up to the moment of his poisoning and his tragic career in Flanders with which the story ends. In the middle is his career as the unbalanced Glass Licenciate. In art, the center panel usually focuses on the "most important" subject matter. For certain narrative purposes, the time he spent as Vidriera stands out above the other two phases of his life. It is usually the stage of delusioned Licentiate that has captured the imagination of the reading public (then and now) for obvious reasons, but in terms of the total narrative message, the flanking parts are as important as the altar centerpiece. (For examples in art of the structure of the triptych, see H. W. Janson, chap. 8, 183, 284 ff.)

The investigations of Kagan into education and the creation of a *letrado* hierarchy focus on a number of factors, many of which can be identified with Rodaja's career and life, and his experiences are illuminated by some of these.[3] Basically, there was a struggle between various classes. A "superior" noble class functioned with great independence because of its means and connections. The latter factor was not an inconsiderable one in the politics and economics of survival in Spain in the two-century period from 1500 to 1700 (Kagan, *Stud.* 175). Family ties proved to be invaluable in the creation and distribution of *letrado* positions. The hierarchies that created and promoted a system of employment became increasingly exclusive, consisting variously of wealthy families and assorted "old boy" networks. As Kagan notes, "The letrado hierarchy also remained

"El licenciado Vidriera"

a hidalgo hierarchy. . . . letrados of 'peasant stock' disappeared, and those from the other end of the social scale were more numerous" (*Stud.* 95).

That the system of appointments was concentrated within a fairly circumscribed circle is obvious. In reviewing aspects of the society of that time, Kagan states:

> This quest for homogeneity, so typical of sixteenth-century Castilian life, tended to sacrifice appointments made solely upon individual merits and skills without regard to birth, blood, or social origin; indeed, in the long run, this quest gradually undermined the ideals set forth by the Catholic kings. (*Stud.* 90)

Cervantes makes his character a licentiate in law. Why did he not choose a character who studied literature or philosophy? One reason is that law was the road to wealth and success. It was considered the best means of obtaining an official appointment (Kagan, *Stud.* 111). Powerful families had accumulated vast wealth, and law, its knowledge and practice, was a key part of that success. The growth and proliferation of the Isabeline, Caroline, and Philippine monarchies created great needs, and the bureaucracies called for knowledgeable people to service them. As Kagan says: "Rare was the college student who, if he outlived his stay at university, did not assume an administrative post. . . . the colegios mayores were also to be the training schools for the university-trained officials of the Spanish crown" (*Stud.* 135).

Law and jurisprudence seemed a good and useful area into which to channel one's talents, especially since the tangible rewards for such study lay within the reach of most students.

> With employment therefore resting upon a university education in jurisprudence, the burden of training the crown's letrados fell directly upon Castile's leading universities: Salamanca and Valladolid. Graduates from these institutions dominated the magistracy and from time to time professors left their university chairs for the more lucrative and honored places offered by the crown. (Kagan, *Stud.* 89)

For a graduate in law, whether a *bachiller, licenciado,* or *doctor,* the number of placement possibilities was larger than one might believe. An appointed position in government was a plum; there were positions to be had in the administration of large and powerful families and as teachers at the universities and colleges; administrators were used in hospitals and in the municipalities (Kagan, *Law* 143). The number of jobs for law graduates therefore seems to have been large, and it becomes a curious question as to why Rodaja, having established himself as a brilliant student, does not fit into the normal pattern that historians have drawn for us. Cristóbal Suárez de Figueroa in *El pasajero* (1617) has a physician give advice to his son concerning his vocational choice: " 'Laws and canons, . . . a noble and illustrious profession, the heart and soul of the cities,' " receives the highest recommendation because of its " 'security of promotions' " (Kagan, *Stud.* 79). Society was generally divided into grandees and titled individuals (many of whom took degrees in law with no intention of practicing it [see Kagan, *Stud.* 37; see also *Law* 190]), the lower classes, and an in-between class of minor bureaucrats and *letrados*. In all cases law was an *entrée* to a better, more stable and lucrative life.[4] The choice of law as a field of study led to many endeavors besides the practice of law. But a particular feature of it, as delineated by José Antonio Maravall, should catch our attention. He notes the presence of "letrados, hombres de saber" from the time of Alfonso el Sabio until Antonio de Guevara as a social class and group (380). For the socially and economically deprived, as we must infer Rodaja was, the choice of law as a field of study must be seen as a way of enjoying the fruits that Philippine society could offer. Yet Cervantes does not have his character graduate beyond a position as servant of the wealthy into one of his own within society. Instead of being one of the "letrados en la ciencia e justicia" (cited by Maravall 380) of whom Mosén Diego de Valera wanted kings to avail themselves, Rodaja becomes a person whose potential is channeled into a mental aberration. This failure is only one of several that can be identified in the career of Tomás Rodaja, Licenciado Vidriera, and Tomás Rueda.

During the Golden Age, studying in Salamanca was the preferred thing to do, and it was the university that offered the best program in law. Attendance at Salamanca brought great prestige and attendant promising career possibilities.

The discovery of the New World and ultra-montagne politics of the Emperor and the several Philips led to the setting up of numerous bodies to dispatch the business of the Empire. As the political order evolved from the universalist program of Charles V to the narrow and closed one of Philip II, a number of contingent things changed too. But changes in structure and form of the government mechanism needed the direction of the right individuals. Jiménez notes on this issue:

> No es extraño, pues, que los españoles más avisados de esa época volvieran con ilusión los ojos hacia las nuevas fundaciones de los Colegios universitarios, que, amparadas por los poderosos, destinadas a los más dignos y disponiendo de cuantiosos medios fundacionales y de hondo prestigio social, trataban de formar una minoría directora, educando a los más capaces para ocupar con provecho en la comunidad puestos de dirección y mando en la gestión de los asuntos del reino y de la Iglesia. (121)[5]

Many of the educational and political programs of the Catholic Kings (and in a different way those of Philip II) were framed in an idealistic way. In time, circumstances and habit modified these efforts, and they degenerated into lesser aims. This is to be seen in the establishment of educational institutions, convents, and other public organizations. As George Addy remarks in his book on the University of Salamanca,

> The dominant impression is one of close allegiance to the status quo, of attempts to distribute limited opportunities to a small and privileged group with scant opportunities for interlopers armed merely with naked merit. (37)[6]

As smaller groups of the advantaged and the privileged became entrenched in the educational institutions, it developed that only the well-to-do could afford all the costs associated with a university degree. Some poor students managed to get an education, but there were expenses that a poor or strapped student could not pay. Marcelin Defourneaux notes that obtaining graduate degrees involved more than just the customary studies. Graduation itself for the licentiate meant the paying of various honoraria, tips to beadles, and the like. For the doctorate there was a dinner, among other supplementary costs, that only the well-to-do could possibly afford (168).[7] Oftentimes these extra costs were reduced slightly by having several

Chapter Three

graduates pool their money to cover the various graduation expenses (Defourneaux 168, 170). This may explain, at least in part, why we are dealing with the *Licenciado* Vidriera and not the *Doctor* Vidriera or for that matter with a *Bachiller* Vidriera. The example of the Bachiller Sansón Carrasco in *Don Quijote* would suffice to show that Cervantes was well aware of the hierarchy of ranks and degrees. So it becomes obvious that the thought of a democratic and egalitarian spirit in the educational milieu in which Rodaja flourished was largely nonexistent, in spite of claims for equality.[8]

In the sixteenth century, as Kamen observes, universities such as Alcalá and Salamanca, which ideally were open for the benefit of all Christians, "began in the sixteenth century to lose their democratic character and to become resorts of the aristocracy. The colleges began to be monopolized by young nobles. Under their influence only those courses that satisfied the needs of the aristocracy were developed" (299–300). Although many books speak of the greatness of Salamanca and Alcalá, the system of education, while outstanding in its visible reality, engendered a high level of discontent.[9]

Individuals who had managed to enter the universities and *colegios mayores* and obtain degrees and eventually step into the world of government, the universities, and church hierarchies came to represent generally at that time a class in themselves, "un nuevo estamento," as Maravall calls it (371). This social class would go through various cycles, with the younger generations profiting from the experience of their elders who had networked with other social and privileged structures. Kagan writes: "And this convergence of interests allowed offspring of the letrado dynasties to enter the colleges on a regular basis. These students, eager for wealth, prestige, and titles of nobility, followed their fathers into the world of office and honor" (*Stud.* 133). The child of *letrados* who was successful had a marked advantage over people like Rodaja, who had no such connection. As Kagan also observes: "The economic problems of the seventeenth century, coupled with increased nepotism, closed off many opportunities for advancement and led to a highlighting of the letrado labor market which affected not only the ruling hierarchies but the learned professions as well" (*Stud.* 104). Also, the idea of a *letrado* class, which was attractive for obvious reasons to the less advantaged individuals of society, was not a pleasant one for everyone. Maravall quotes Hernando del Pulgar, who focused on some disadvantages:

> Vemos por experiencia... algunos omnes destos que iudgamos nacidos de baxa sangre forçarles su natural inclinación a dexar los oficios baxos de los padres, e aprender ciencia e ser grandes letrados. (382)

While the educational system promoted some features of social and economic mobility, it could also be viewed as a threat to other middle-level *estamentos* and in some ways created dependencies with the nobles and noble class that might have proved ultimately problematic. Fires of resentment were no doubt fueled by watching the privileged advance in the professions thanks to friends and influence:

> Exploiting their friends on the Royal Council, colegiales moved regularly into teaching positions and official posts. Promotion was almost automatic, and it was common knowledge that the son or nephew of a government official who obtained a *beca* ... would have a secure political future. (Kagan, *Stud.* 101)

A further example of the decline of values in the universities was the election of university officials. In these the merit of the individual was not always the deciding factor in the vote, and there are numerous examples of irregularities in plumping for the votes of the students (cf. Kagan, *Stud.* 137–38). These failures of values in favor of nepotism, a closed view of values in education, suspicion of professors in questions of orthodoxy, the censorship of books, as Kamen notes of Salamanca (83), can be viewed as a by-product of the general trend of values during the reign of Philip II with its hostility toward new ideas. (See Defourneaux 176 for the development of these ideas.) It is clear that social mobility, economic progress, and advancement were seriously restricted to a few limited groups, and for this reason, Rodaja's history, with his brilliant performance in law at Salamanca but without any *destino* other than delusion and madness, demands clarification and explanation. His obscure origins may cue the attentive reader to his inability to secure a position that would enable him to obtain the goal he had set for himself.[10]

El Saffar views Rodaja as a failure, someone who "cannot make meaningful contact with society" (*Novel to Romance* 60). If Tomás Rodaja is a failure, it is not because "he cannot transform his surroundings into meaningful abstract forms" (El Saffar, *Novel to Romance* 60), but rather, as history shows, because the society in which he lives and flourishes is rife with various forms of social ostracism, corruption brought about by nepotism and cronyism, social structures ossified into tools for advancement based on wealth and lineage (see below). Rodaja's failure is the failure of a commoner who seeks to achieve *fama* through education and the field of law, normally the passport to advancement, wealth, and position. His odyssey from poverty to mental delusion and finally to death can only be viewed as the real and symbolic failure of his political and social environment, which makes the idea of economic and social advancement something of a cruel joke.

One sure bar to social and economic advancement was to be suspected of being a *converso*. The informed reader cannot forget the example of Fray Luis de León, the professor at the University of Salamanca, a *converso* (as were his persecutors) who suffered imprisonment at the hands of the Inquisitors. His background could not have been a help to him.[11] Given some of the statutes and mores of university life, his presence on the faculty of Salamanca is a testimony to two interesting facts: statutes of lineage prevented people with "obscure origins" from occupying university positions, and given this rule, their presence is a testimony to the wiliness of *conversos* in penetrating the university world. In fact, considering the official attitudes toward *cristianos nuevos* (and I think of Luis de León as a splendid example), it must have been a hazardous undertaking to approach certain features of classical learning. A person studying the Bible had to study three languages: Greek, Latin, and Hebrew (Jiménez 177). An affinity for Hebrew may have attracted the attention of the Inquisitors (some of whom were *ex illis* themselves).

The hostile attitude toward *conversos* that permeated all aspects of Spanish life, including university life, may yield some insights into what I refer to as Vidriera's "failure." Defourneaux offers a very insightful quote on this subject:

"El licenciado Vidriera"

A Franciscan teacher of the university of Salamanca at the end of the sixteenth century wrote on behalf of several colleagues:

> We came to Spain to avoid the doctrine that being a blasphemer, a thief, or highwayman, or an adulterer, or being guilty of sacrilege and any other vices, was better than having Jewish origin. Our ancestors embraced the Christian faith two or three centuries ago. But there remains an intolerable intolerance [sic]: suppose that there are two candidates for a professorship, a benefice, a prelature, or some other office. One is a gifted man who comes from a family which was once Jewish but turned Christian ages ago. The other is illiterate, ungifted, but simply because he is an "old Christian," he will be preferred to the other." (38)[12]

This quote clearly shows the prejudice and bias *conversos* felt. There were more biases. In order to get into a *colegio mayor* one had to show that one was of Old Christian stock (Kagan, *Stud.* 109). A passage from Diego de Torres Villarroel (cited by Addy) supports this contention: "Collegian: There's no career in church or state *Sans* proof of pedigree" (61). Addy also says in this respect, "Furthermore, no persons of 'fame in the world' were acceptable, nor could any person of Jewish descent, no matter how remote, be admitted" (57).

In a religion- and "race"-conscious world, the "pleitos de hidalguía" served numerous functions. Aside from avoiding the stigma of New Christianity, they served as an exemption from royal taxation (Kagan, *Law* 11). But the obsession with *limpieza* demonstrated just how permeated Spanish society was with New Christians who had assimilated into the various levels of life and society. Kamen shows how statutes of *limpieza* created barriers for applicants to the college of San Bartolomé in Salamanca (119). A similar statute was adopted on 23 July 1547, in Toledo. These laws, which were followed by the church and educational institutions, paradoxically came to be prejudicial to many nobles and people "of quality." Such a statute did not go without complaint from these nobles (123). Put more precisely,

> As Silíceo and his opponents well knew, few members of the nobility had not been tainted with converso blood. By promoting a *limpieza* statute, therefore, the archbishop was obviously claiming for his own class a racial purity which the tainted nobility could not boast. (Kamen 124)

Chapter Three

More particularly applicable to the world in which Rodaja moves, in 1573 a decree excluded *conversos* from holding teaching positions (Kagan, *Stud.* 11). This brings us closer to our hypothesis and vision of the reason for Tomás Rodaja's inability to find a niche for himself in Spanish life, in spite of his brilliance. (See Kagan, *Stud.* 90-91, for an example of someone who did not get a post because of being a *converso*.)

Rodaja studies in Salamanca thanks to the generosity of his masters. His economic condition would not have allowed him the possibility of study without the benefit of some assistance. To receive a scholarship in a *colegio mayor,* one had to pass a long and costly investigation into one's *limpieza* (Kagan, *Stud.* 130), and ultimately, these scholarships were given to people of the highest Old Christianity. Perhaps Rodaja could neither have afforded nor withstood such scrutiny.

The legal profession, as Kagan avers, had become a suspect one.

> One drawback for the profession, however, was a lack of social status and prestige. Advocates were letrados and respected as such, but because it was an open profession, many Jewish converts to Catholicism (*conversos*) were admitted to practice long after the church and the magistracy had debarred New Christians and others accused of not admitting to having Jewish or Moorish blood. Owing to the profusion of conversos, the profession was considered to be "tainted" and its notorious lack of blood purity only encouraged those who believed that advocates did little more than fleece the public at large. (Kagan, *Law* 71)

Kagan (*Law* 190-91) also points out that judges from powerful mercantile families were associated with the *converso* and New Christian taint. Such *conversos* were to be avoided because they could not be counted on for the best advice. In 1683, Melchor de Cabrera Núñez, in a work of his, told why he wanted lawyers to be of Old Christian blood: " 'the descendants of Jews are inconstant in matters of faith, of bad customs, overly ambitious, seditious, usurious, and the capital enemies of Christ and of Christianity'" (cited by Kagan, *Law* 74).[13] While there is no specific evidence in the text that Vidriera is of *converso* stock, I have entered into this question here because I link the

"El licenciado Vidriera"

proscriptions toward *conversos* with the fact that Vidriera makes no social progress in spite of his choice of a profession that offered great possibilities for advancement. Being a commoner or a poor farmer does not seem to be *enough* to have prevented Vidriera's rise.

There is yet another reason to account for the possible "suspension" of Rodaja as a brilliant licentiate in law. If he was without any possibilities, what else was left to him but to emigrate to the New World? However, as Kagan points out, such licentiates would not go abroad since "the crown banned all lawyers from its New Colony in Peru" (19).[14]

In essence, Rodaja's lack of progress and social and economic mobility in Spain may very well be explained by the possibility that he was a *converso* or from a family tainted by New Christian blood. This would make Rodaja a person suffering from more than one strike against him in Spanish life: coming from a poor family in a society in which the well-to-do had the greatest advantages and, on top of that, having important avenues of social progress closed off by racial prejudice.[15] This last ingredient may provide the reason why this brilliant person, endowed with an acute intelligence and the ambition to obtain honor through his intellect, goes nowhere in that society.

Amezúa divides Cervantes's stories into two phases: the *satírico* and the *novelístico*, "El licenciado Vidriera" is relegated to the former (2: 182–84). Casalduero also focuses on the satirical element, noting that the story contains various kinds of criticism. Cervantes's purpose, according to Casalduero, is to have the whole gamut of human endeavor file by our eyes (110–11). Forcione, in his treatment of the story, notes this important feature of Cervantes's handling of the satire motif: "As a critic the licentiate is obsessed with man's evil and hypocrisy, sees them in absolute clarity, and exposes them mercilessly" (263). That Cervantes has turned to satire to focus on the foibles and evils of humankind is without doubt. Most interestingly for my own analysis, Forcione identifies Vidriera with a Renaissance tradition of "misdirected scholars" (305). Moreover, Forcione associates an important aspect of Vidriera with the problem of knowledge. Vidriera's tale is "the tale of a failed education" (305).[16]

81

Chapter Three

In order to study the satire one must return to the basic structural principle of the tale that I pointed out in the beginning of the chapter, i.e., the tale as a triptych. The initial phase is represented by the left, adjoining panel. It comprises the joining of Rodaja with the wealthy students, his education, and his illness and partial recovery, and the emergence of the "diseased licentiate," to use Forcione's term (305). At this point we are at the central focus of the character. But at the same time Cervantes has endowed the triptych with a progressive rhythm that is cumulative. Consequently, we cannot and should not look at Vidriera as an isolated character. Likewise, in the last phase, the final right panel will be the conclusion of the first two parts and not a mere insignificant appendage without a link with the earlier events. Therefore, I must add a qualifier to Forcione's view of the satire of Vidriera. If Vidriera is obsessed with "man's evil and hypocrisy . . . and exposes them mercilessly" (263), it is because his obsession is a product of the very society that upheld the values of a preferential and well-to-do order over the ideal political and Christian notion that all beings are equal in the eyes of God. Education in this society departed from the early liberal and democratic values of equality of the mind and the ideal of learning, values that were undermined, in part, by Philip II's policies of purity of blood (see Kagan, *Law* 157). These and other policies of Philip II are inferentially present throughout the *Novelas ejemplares,* as a backdrop to the tales. José Antonio Fernández Santamaría notes, regarding the University of Alcalá de Henares (and his comments are equally applicable to Salamanca): "It is only after the passing of the age of Erasmus and the coming of the age of Trent that dogmatism begins to permeate and hamper the flexibility of the orthodox purview" (4). Defourneaux views the waning of academic life and its causes as a consequence of "Spain's increasing introversion ever since the time of Philip II: hostility to all new ideas, and a regression to the methods and the spirit of scholasticism, after the flowering of the first half of the sixteenth century had withered away" (176). The reign, then, of Philip II and the early years of the reign of Philip III are at the core of Cervantes's disillusion and dissatisfaction. The decline of Spanish society, its universities, the military and naval establishment, and the various mores that supported and encouraged the

"El licenciado Vidriera"

policies of Philip II are, to judge from the various creations of Cervantes, the responsible parties for the sad state of affairs.

Closely related to the satirical principle of the central portion of the "El licenciado Vidriera" triptych is the picaresque literary phenomenon. Rodríguez Luis believes that a "picaresque awareness" as a genre is created by the use of recognizable characters, topoi, and a location: "Es claro que Cervantes debía tener muy en cuenta en este principio de su novela la historia del *Lazarillo de Tormes,* con la intención de establecer un contraste entre el primer pícaro y su Tomás Rodaja" (1: 193–94). Rodríguez Luis perceptively homes in on the basic principle of the picaresque. Moreover, he also associates the tale—as I believe must be done to understand a basic impulse in the creation of *Las novelas ejemplares*—with the popularity of the *Guzmán de Alfarache,* and draws attention to similarities with the *Buscón:*

> El objeto de su [Cervantes's] visión es, sin embargo, la maldad y la corrupción del hombre; el mismo, por lo tanto, de la picaresca. Porque en esta censura de la vida de la época, el autor está verdaderamente dibujando el contenido intelectual, el esqueleto, por decirlo así, de una novela picaresca despojada de la acción que podría poner en movimiento en característica visión del mundo. La descarnada crítica de Tomás, incluído el humor—ausente, en general, del *Guzmán,* pero desbordante en el *Buscón*—, es en esencia semejante a la del pícaro, aunque potenciada en su caso por la vocación intelectual del crítico y por la ausencia de contacto directo con la realidad, gracias a ser de vidrio del licenciado y a tener, por lo tanto, que rehuir cualquier contacto con la gente que no sea oral. (1: 201–02)

Forcione also touches on the Quevedian link, which I think is fundamental in this story:

> He [Cervantes] could already see the spirit of the Licenciado Vidriera clearly emerging in the literary and cultural life of Spain—the nightmarish fantasies of Quevedesque satire, as well as in the desolate vision of the popular picaresque narratives, with the panoramic surveys of human failings, their cultivation of railing abuse, and their antagonistic engagement with their readers. (292–93)

Chapter Three

As Tomás Rodaja evolves into the delusioned Licenciado Vidriera, one of his manifestations is the recital of aphorisms. One aspect of this behavior can be identified with the picaresque literary tradition. The *Lazarillo* excoriated certain levels of life, which the *Guzmán de Alfarache* also censured, with an accompanying plethora of moral commentary. The *Buscón* returns to a depiction of the various stations of life, with its occupations and trades, but within the same type of narrative presentation as the *Lazarillo* (in spite of some *infrarrealismo*). But the *Buscón* is only one phase of Francisco de Quevedo's dealing with the social satire: in the *Sueños* his treatment of the subject is similar to that of "El licenciado Vidriera." This same tendency is seen in Luis Vélez de Guevara's *El diablo cojuelo*. There is in the presentation of the social satirical vision of "El licenciado Vidriera" a social tangibility found in the *Sueños*.

The issue of criticism coming out of the mouth of a seemingly "crazy" man has been associated with a number of biblical, classical, and Renaissance phenomena. While this line of argument may have affirmed the opinions of some critics, it has also clouded the issue. The words *mad, crazy,* and *insane* are generally to be found in discussions of "El licenciado Vidriera." The comparison with Don Quijote is inevitable, making Cervantes a creator of madmen (cf. Amezúa 2: 167). However, for Marcelino Menéndez Pelayo, Vidriera's madness was "adventicia" and secondary (cited by Amezúa 2: 173). Amezúa also offers the following explanation:

> que para Cervantes es preferible ser loco a estar cuerdo, como un supremo e irritante fracaso de la razón humana, como si a ésta no le estuviera permitido decir verdad alguna, y para poder proferirlas, tuviese que renunciar a la luz de la razón y sumirse fatalmente en el abismo tenebroso y mísero de la demencia. (2: 186–87)

For Forcione, Vidriera's madness is associated with "the moral, philosophical, and literary themes of the work," yet mixed with the visionary's wish to penetrate the illusions of others with their follies and vices (241).

The term *loco,* with its variant, *locura,* is used by critics in a somewhat indiscriminate manner.[17] In a strict clinical schema Vidriera is not so much mad, or insane; this would imply a disconnection with reality. He sees reality very clearly (albeit with his own preferred view of that reality). Vidriera suffers from a delusional disorder of a somatic type, but as I hope to show, given the nature of some of his criticism, a delusional disorder of the grandiose type that involves a certain identity or a special relationship to a deity or famous person.[18] My approach to Vidriera's mental state after he ate the poisoned fruit, his illness, and his final emergence as a mentally afflicted being is psychological in nature and implies an acknowledgment of Vidriera's own past experiences as I have been interpreting them.

Nothing, of course, occurs without some social etiology in the work. I am positing the possibility that Vidriera's final convalescence, which involves his delusion, is not accidental, but part of a vision that is carefully crafted by Cervantes.[19] Why does Vidriera emerge from his illness with this strange behavioral problem? He could easily have been cured of the toxic effects of the poison to resume his life as a licentiate in law, but Cervantes wishes to utilize the motif of derangement for other purposes.

The scholar's temptation to look for sources in Cervantes's literary and cultural present and past has yielded, to say the least, some interesting results. Predictably some investigations have been fruitful and others have led nowhere. All of this attests both to the complexity of the tale and the complexity of the figure of the Licentiate. He brings together a number of symbols, threads, and metaphors that have plentiful echoes in contemporary and earlier cultures. Basically, his figure involves light, glass, knowledge, learning, wisdom, and social satire.

A number of classical writers have offered similar themes. In Book 6 of the *Aeneid* we see the motif of God speaking through the sibyl. Herodotus similarly shows us this motif at the shrine of Apollo at Delphi. Macrobius deals with his dream visions. Lucian, in his *Philosophies for Sale,* can offer some useful contacts with our tale and this phase of the character. Plato presents the notion of God speaking through poets.

The Renaissance abounds in works that deal with aphorisms, maxims, and *sententiae.* Certainly Licenciado Vidriera's salient trait during this part of the tale is his recital of short, pithy, sometimes witty aphorisms. The writings of Juvenal and

Chapter Three

Martial, of Hesiod and Theogonus are called to mind. The presence of apothegms during the Renaissance, principally in the figure of Erasmus, would corroborate the fact that Cervantes is dealing with a tradition that is fairly well known and accepted in his time. Since many of the Licentiate's statements entail aspects of the use of human reason, one could cite Heraclitus and his notion of the presence of *logos* as a universal principle as well as the unmasking of a false view of the world. In *De Sensu,* Aristotle discusses the material of the universe, of light and the senses, which, given the links of the Licentiate with the idea of glass and light, could be seen as a link as well with Nicholas of Cusa's *De Docta Ignorantia,* but with certain limitations (just as Tiresias dispenses prophecies but is not mentally deranged in any way). Forcione speaks of Licenciado Vidriera and his link with the school of Cynics: as a Cynic, Vidriera represents that tendency among philosophers of that school to be "demaskers" of evil and foolishness (247). However, at the same time Forcione believes that Cervantes has presented Vidriera as a "flawed philosopher" (263), and in detaching himself from Vidriera, Cervantes is exposing the limitations of Vidriera's vision (see also Huarte de San Juan, as outlined in Johnson's *Madness and Lust*).

I save for last the links with biblical literature, some of which may be particularly applicable. Without a doubt the Book of Proverbs can offer numerous links with the Glass Licentiate: its own pithy maxims; its focus on fools and foolishness; the personified figure of wisdom; the avoidance of evil ways; the imprecations against adultery; the relations between father and son, man and wife; the avoidance of immoral and loose women, false witnesses, pride, and arrogance; the pursuit of righteousness in the face of foolishness and immorality; the avoidance of slander, the cruel, and the wicked; the pursuit of truth and avoidance of deceit and falsehood; the search for good companionship; the avoidance of arrogance and faithlessness, excessive wine bibbing, flattery and flatterers, lying; and others. What is particularly interesting and applicable is the social setting with which the Book of Proverbs opens, and this is very reminiscent of the "El licenciado Vidriera":

> Wisdom cries aloud in the *street;* / in the *markets* she raises her / voice; / on the top of the *walls* she cries / out; / at the

> entrance of the city gates / she speaks. . . . (Prov. 1.20–21; emphasis mine)

A second element is the pursuit of wisdom in Proverbs that relates to Vidriera as social critic.

In Ecclesiasticus we find the same concern with wisdom and the excoriation of vices, many of which are closely identified with a social context: reprobation of lies and lying; the suffering of fools; thievery; fornication; the breaking of marriage vows; good, loyal, and evil wives; false accusations, deceptions, slandering; the love between father and son; jealousy; anger; love of lucre; excessive wine bibbing; bribes; and injustice. There is, however, a dimension to Ecclesiasticus that I consider crucially important for its link with this aspect of "El licenciado Vidriera." The writer(s) emphasize the speech act as an important means of communication, on both spiritual matters and worldly ones:

> For wisdom is known through / speech, / and education through words / of the tongue. . . . (Ecclus. 4.24)

And as if in anticipation of the very creation and communication of the tale itself:

> Be ready to listen to every / narrative / and do not let wise proverbs / escape you. (Ecclus. 6.35)

The act of the formulation of the maxims and *sententiae* is concealed by the often clever and witty remark:

> The mark of a happy heart is a / cheerful face, / but to devise proverbs requires / painful thinking. (Ecclus. 13.26)

Vidriera's cleverness may cover up the psychological substratum of this phase of his development, which, I contend, is linked with aspects of his previous existence. Most importantly, it is Vidriera's new role as "sage" that brings us into contact with the most immediate problem of human intercourse: language.

> *The wise man makes himself / beloved through his words,* / but the courtesies of fools are / wasted. (Ecclus. 20.13; emphasis mine)

Chapter Three

In the writings of Paul,[20] one sees the same preoccupation with wisdom and the acknowledgment of the presence of folly. In 1 Corinthians, Paul proposes that one should become a fool for Christ, recommending the utilization of foolishness for spiritual means. Paul underscores the value of married life (6.10–12). He also mentions the ability of talking like a madman (or a fool) in order to say meaningful, wise things (3.18–19, 4.10). The only difference I see is that Paul suggests the use of foolishness for Christly purposes, while Cervantes may be using this only superficially (see below on this idea).

Even Paul understands the importance of the socioverbal contact. He says, "To one is given through the spirit the utterance of wisdom, and to another the utterance of knowledge according to the same spirit" (1 Cor. 12.8). In 14.6 Paul concedes the importance of the linguistic key to communication, adding,

> So with yourselves; if you in a tongue utter speech that is not intelligible, how will any one know what is said? For you will be speaking into the air. There are doubtless many different languages in the world, and none is without meaning; but if I do not know the meaning of the language, I shall be a foreigner to the speaker and the speaker a foreigner to me. (1 Cor. 14.9–11).

Vidriera does not retire to a monastery to contemplate in an ascetic manner the evils and foibles of this world in favor of the other world. He sets out through the streets, in the plazas and market places. He talks to all; he attracts everyone who wants to ply him with questions in search of his witty, clever, and wise answers.

Of the various proposed sources, I find the biblical ones very strongly suggestive and closer to what we read in Cervantes because they highlight the social content of the advice and maxims, and at the same time strongly explore the relationship between Vidriera and language in a social context.

The idea of Tomás Rodaja as a "glass" licentiate calls for an explanation as to why Cervantes chose this phenomenon for his character. For Casalduero, the fear Rodaja had of being made of glass was a part of his fear of death (118). Acknowledging his fragility (242), his "glassiness," for Forcione, is "symbolic of the keen insight into which he is gifted and the freedom of a man totally dedicated to the spirit" (241). That the vitrine feature of his person is seen as a means is fairly generally acknowledged. Forcione brings in the possibility of seeing light in this tale as "the satire of light," of the "light of Diogenes's lamp of truth with the charity of Christ" (296).[21]

The motif of the delusion of glass is intimately linked with the metaphor of life and the instrument for the unmasking of evil and foolishness. I submit that it would be useful to study Cervantes's creation of glass and light in the view of other contemporary Spanish creations. Santa Teresa, who often assumes the role of fool for God, makes ample use of both motifs of madness and light. The latter she links with God. Light is His light, which illuminates her spirit. His light is His word, and all that she does achieves greater meaning and clarification because of such light.

For a reading public aware of the writings of Santa Teresa (and other writers who use the motif of light in a religious way), it was inevitable for them to "read" the glass/light motif in religious terms. But Cervantes's character, in his glassy state, keeps the reflection on a purely secular level. The maxims and aphorisms he utters tend to explore human relationships. The "vitrine" nature, symbolically, of the character allows the perceptions to filter through his person/intellect to be passed on to others, whence the satirical nature of this phase of his life.

Amezúa on the one hand, quoting Narciso Alonso Cortés, views the aphorisms as being part of the Renaissance gusto for maxims and *sententiae* (173–74).[22] Yet he denies that they are strictly speaking apothegms. He rather sees them as quick touches, "dictados por un Juez que los pronuncia por sí solo" (186). Casalduero sees this phase of Vidriera's life with its aphorisms and *dichos* as representing the nucleus of the tale (110). Closer to my interpretation is the view of El Saffar, who sees the aphoristic phase in "degenerative" terms:

> The Licentiate fails both in life and letters. In life he cannot make meaningful contact with society. He has no friends outside of the intellectual community and finds only sickness and death in alternating roles. But in letters he fails also, for he cannot transform his surroundings into meaningful abstract forms. His intellectual activity is reduced to

Chapter Three

> the production of only occasionally witty aphorisms. His is an unrelieved story of estrangement in which the main protagonist is shown only in roles of conflict with his environment. (*Novel to Romance* 60)

I agree with the notions she expresses of failure (although for different reasons) and estrangement, but also point out that this phase is a carefully structured one in which the Licentiate turns his back on the society in which, as a brilliant but poor student and failed professional, he has tried to succeed. The metamorphosis from rational law licentiate to irrational and deluded person may also be associated with other psychological processes. Basic to his obsession and state is the delusion that he is made of glass.[23] I contend that the resurfacing of Rodaja as the deluded and deranged scholar represents the unleashing of a suppressed (and possibly repressed) part of himself. As a poor student his career depended upon the charity of those wealthier and more powerful than he. His humble station in life largely limited his success on a social and economic scale. This process of failure could not have had a positive effect on someone who moved in an historical atmosphere not given to allowing the expression of one's dissatisfaction (except, as in the case of Cervantes, through writing). What is important in the study of the aphorisms is to see that what Vidriera does is to lash out at his society in a castigating way, something he did not do in his "rational" state. It may well be that certain critical tendencies were repressed, and it is during his vitrine state of mental disequilibrium that these repressed matters rise to the surface of his consciousness. Sitting in judgment of his society is basically a messianic as well as a defensive act. Having failed to achieve the normal successes usually accorded to a brilliant individual, Vidriera's brilliance becomes now, in his glassy state, a whip with which to flagellate the society that keeps him hovering at the edges of success that his poverty and perhaps religious background prevent him from obtaining. Cervantes, as a critic of this and many other social ills present during the reigns of the early Hapsburgs, has cleverly placed his own criticism in the mouth of a deranged and obsessed hanger-on of the court, a failed lawyer. In such a guise, Cervantes can amply indulge his own deep feelings of failure and inadequacy as someone whose heroism and devotion to the crown met with no substantial reward. Like Rodaja, Cervantes achieved no visible success as *alcabalero* or in the other endeavors of his life. Denied the opportunity to emigrate to the New World (because of being a *converso?*) in order to achieve the success that so eluded him in Spain, Cervantes is reduced to channeling his anger, bitterness, and disappointment into a literary act. Vidriera's sickness is an effective weapon in Cervantes's hands because it cleverly conceals the true, revelatory psychological process at work both in the character and in the author.

As part of his Counter-Reformation vision of later sixteenth- and seventeenth-century Spanish literature, Casalduero could not help but interpret several key incidents in the life of Rodaja through a religious light. It must have been very tempting to associate the poisoned quince with the Garden of Eden (a temptation, moreover, to which he succumbs), for he says:

> No es el pecado de la carne, el mundo sensual frente al mundo del espíritu; es el pecado de la inteligencia. Tomás rechaza a la mujer, pero come de la fruta que ella ofrece, un membrillo del árbol del bien y del mal. (118)[24]

Casalduero also extends his concern with the question of Vidriera's supposed symbol of knowledge to another area: "armas y letras" (see also below). He sees: "El pecado de la inteligencia queda encerrado en ese marco de eternidad y gloria, de inmortalidad con que había soñado siempre Cervantes: las Armas y las Letras" (119). Much has been said of Vidriera as a philosopher and his identification with the question of knowledge. El Saffar is correct when she interprets Vidriera's knowledge as a means of disarming "reality of its persistent corrosion of life and health and personal integrity" (*Novel to Romance* 57). But I believe that she overextends her argument to see Vidriera's view as paradigmatic of all human knowledge, or even of his need to transpose everything into an "abstract, generalized formula" (59). If, as she contends, "he cannot make meaningful contact with society" and has "no friends outside of the intellectual community" (60), it is because his own radius of activity has been generally within the circumscribed area of university life. As a poor student dependent upon the charity of wealthier students, his affirmation of self would be greater within the university world, where we are led to believe that, *ideally,* talent counts (but in a practical way, to judge from Vidriera's outcome, we see that it does not). Rather than speak of a crisis or polemic of knowledge, which is far too broad, we must speak of learning, and here I also see where Cervantes's criticism enters. The subsumed question of knowledge is something like the following: What is the value of Rodaja's learning if it limits him to being a poor but brilliant student and does not translate itself into more tangible rewards?[25]

To return to the concept of the tripartite structure of the work, it is in the central panel of the triptych that another element enters: the public one. By public I mean Rodaja's placement into a wider social context than before in his student period. The resultant product is a prose that is more functionally visible than before. Newer and wider dimensions are created by having Vidriera travel through social space; he loses the "flatness" as a character that he has in the first phase of the story, where he made a spectacle of himself. In fact, Vidriera is a "spectacle" (I use the word in a theatrical and dramaturgical sense). His question/response/counterresponse banter with the people is an example of theater within the prose presentation. This feature is a parody of the rhetorical questioning style of teaching.[26]

The final observation to be made on this tale concerns the "armas y letras" motif and its link with the final panel of the triptych, which presents the death of Rueda on the fields of Flanders. This theme was developed even more fully in *Don Quijote,* which caused Casalduero to comment that these motifs "encierran un cuadro social" (109).[27]

Perhaps justifying Rueda's joining the troops in Flanders, Defourneaux notes, "For the honour of their country, the graduates of Salamanca and Alcalá reinforced the officers and men of the *tercios*" (163). The Licenciado Tomás Castro y Aguila (1649) compares advocates to soldiers, which may also illuminate aspects of Rueda's choice to go to Flanders: "'Advocates fight for and defend the state with letters, the soldiers with their arms'" (cited by Kagan, *Law* 74). This is exactly what Rueda does.

Geoffrey Parker uses a quote from *Don Quijote* (2.24), which may focus more exactly on why Rueda goes to Flanders. Having lost any chances of success in the court, and having lost

"El licenciado Vidriera"

all interest for his fellow townspeople, Rueda is left more than ever without any resources:

> —A la guerra me lleva mi necesidad;
> Si tuviera dineros, no fuera en verdad. (40n1)

Because of its brevity, this somewhat laconic ending to the tale contained in the right side of the triptych is largely ignored, especially after the lengthier and more developed center panel—Vidriera's career as resident madman. But the brief description of his demise, by its very nature, conceals Cervantes's final criticism, which is of a political, social, and economic nature. It is, of course, also the final step in Rodaja's cycle toward failure. His death ensures his career as *fracasado*. The war alluded to is the 80-year uprising in the Low Countries, which was an uprising of both a political and a religious nature. As we have seen previously in other chapters, politics in the Spain of Philip II and Philip III is closely involved with religion, and vice-versa. Cervantes had never been to Flanders nor to France, for that matter, as Amezúa notes (2: 179), but it is the historical and political character of the event that must have caught his attention.

Parker, in his book on this period of Spanish history, opens his investigation by noting that this war never captured the interest of Spanish historians, precisely because of its meaning in Spanish history.[28] This was a war which deeply involved a sense of honor for Spain; to have lost it or to have abandoned it constituted a serious and flagrant humiliation to its power.[29] Quite aside from the notion of national honor, there was the question of the cost to Spain of such a war. Parker notes that in the face of objections, "These isolated voices of doom had little impact. On the whole there were few in Spain prepared to admit the possibility that the war in the Netherlands could go on indefinitely and *that its cost could prove too great for the treasury to bear* [emphasis mine]" (135).[30] There are at the same time some features to the handling of the war with overwhelming moral implications. Spain had adopted a mind-set toward the war that did not admit any palliatives with respect to the outcome.[31] In fact, it was this notion of political obstinacy that must have crushed the hopes of Spaniards. It was not

Chapter Three

just the overwhelming costs of this protracted and unwinnable war that must have impressed the public, who, ultimately through taxes and other levies, became the victims at home of these enterprises. But it was the absurdity of having to reason that war, with its loss of life and damage to the economy of the country, was more acceptable than peace:

> This consistent refusal to make concessions brings us closer to the real reasons which underlay Spain's persistent use of force in the Netherlands. It was felt that peace would be more damaging than war, and in the sixteenth century a peace which involved religious as well as political concessions were especially suspect. (Parker 131–32)

Consequently, Rueda's death must be examined within the particular meaning that the war in Flanders had in Spain at the time. Cervantes's deliberate choice of locale accentuates precisely the influence and impact of that war. Given the political and economic considerations of the uprising on Spanish life, Rueda's death becomes even more significant and symbolic, especially within the ironic design that lies at the base of the tale.

In conclusion, in the composition of the work, Cervantes chooses a character who, from the first, is presented to us within an economic and social structure—a poor, low-level individual who through his acute and gifted intelligence manages to be educated in an environment not particularly hospitable to the advancement and social mobility of the poor and even prejudiced in favor of the wealthy and well-to-do. He earns the *Licenciatura* in Law, one of the most potentially rewarding degrees available, yet does not obtain any of the promised rewards. Poisoned by a jealous woman, he emerges from his illness with a defective mental condition, imagining himself to be made of glass but at the same time capable of offering wise insights about life. Once cured, he loses the ability to recite maxims and equally loses the interest he held for other people. Left with no possibilities, he goes to Flanders as a soldier, where he achieves "fame" by dying. Thus concludes the cycle of life of this poor boy who "made good." His first failure is not to move ahead in a society where social and economic advancement was strongly conditioned by status, lineage, wealth, and powerful

"El licenciado Vidriera"

connections and friends. His status as deluded madman reflects his inability and failure to be a constructive part of his society, but only a "hazmerreír," becoming the butt of jokes by the people surrounding him. His knowledge and wisdom are largely lost on his own society. Lastly, his death in a dubious political and religious enterprise must have been for Cervantes the ultimate fate of a person such as this. He ironically buries all his intelligence, potential, and promise on the battlefields of Flanders. In this view, never was there a greater *fracaso* than that of Tomás Rodaja, Licenciado Vidriera, and Tomás Rueda.

Chapter Four

The Prose of Honor

It is my belief that some of the *novelas ejemplares* were written either as a "lectura anti-alemaniana" or as a "lectura anti-lopesca." The first was a response to Mateo Alemán's importance as a contemporary prose writer and his authorship of one of the true "best-sellers" of its time. The second, the "lectura anti-lopesca," is explained by the tremendous popularity of Lope in his own time compared with Cervantes's as a dramatist. No one today could see Cervantes, the playwright, as a worthy competitor to Lope, but there is ample evidence to believe that they viewed each other as rivals. There are specific events to corroborate the history of this enmity between the two men. The personal problem began rather early, as Federico Carlos Sáinz de Robles notes, around 1602, when Jerónimo Velázquez and Cervantes met. Cervantes had hoped that Velázquez would put on his plays (see Tómov 618). In a letter, dated 4 August 1604, Lope gives voice to his feelings: " 'De poetas no digo: buen siglo es éste. Muchos en cierne para el año que viene; pero ninguno hay tan malo como Cervantes ni tan necio que alabe a Don Quijote' " (cited by de Torre 46). According to Sáinz de Robles, Lope had three kinds of enemies: Aristotelians, Gongoristas, and those "dolorosos de la gloria," and Cervantes belonged, according to him, to the last group (Tómov 619). In the prologue to *Don Quijote,* part 1, Cervantes refers to the "caterva de filósofos," which is supposedly an indirect reference to Lope's *Peregrino.* Furthermore, in chapter 48 of *Don Quijote,* part 1, the canon says, concerning *comedias:*

> "estas [comedias] que ahora se usan, así las imaginadas como las de historia, todas o las más son conocidos disparates y cosas que no llevan pies ni cabeza, y, con todo eso, el vulgo las oye con gusto, y las tiene y las aprueba por buenas,

> estando tan lejos de serlo; y los autores que las representan dicen que así han de ser, porque así las quiere el vulgo, y no de otra manera... pero como las comedias se han hecho mercadería vendible, dicen, y dicen verdad, que los representantes no se las comprarían si no fuesen de aquel jaez; y así, el poeta procura acomodarse con lo que el representante que le ha de pagar su obra le pide." (Cited by Tómov 622–23)

Antonie Van Beysterveldt, recalling the canon's discourse, notes: "toutes les comedias représentées, non seulement à la Cour mais dans toute l'Espagne, devraient être soumises à une censure sévère. Toute comedia ne répondant pas aux préceptes des Anciens devrait être interdite" (8). Lope does offer some praise for Cervantes: " 'no le faltó gracia y estilo a Miguel de Cervantes,' " thinking of *Las novelas ejemplares.* Yet he qualifies this statement by describing *Las novelas ejemplares* as " 'libros de grande entretenimiento' pero para no traicionar al adjetivo debieran ser obra de 'hombres científicos,' de rica experiencia" (cited by Rico 10). As a final note to the problem, suffice it to say that while Lope saw all his plays mounted, Cervantes never lived to see any presented. Juan Bautista Avalle-Arce, in "Lope de Vega and Cervantes," notes the keen competition between Lope and Cervantes and suggests that the *Novelas a Marcia Leonarda* was Lope's answer to Cervantes on the art of the short story. Van Beysterveldt is more precise about Cervantes's reaction toward rivals and peers. Speaking of the difference between theory and practice in Cervantes's dramaturgy, he says:

> Cette divergence entre la théorie et la pratique—que Schack le premier a mise en relief en étudiant les conceptions dramatiques de Cervantes—, fait penser que l'irritation du grand écrivain contre le théâtre de son époque était causée, non pas par le spectacle des transgressions continuelles des "règles," mais plutôt par l'envie que lui inspiraient les éclatants succès des dramaturges de son temps. (8)

Cervantes had to live with the enormous success that Lop achieved as the most important and most popular dramatist c his time. Cervantes's plays pale alongside the quality of Lope' prodigious dramatic production. It is obvious that Cervante cannot compete with Lope for the adulation of the publi Moreover, Lope's formula for the *comedia* is based upon h

The Prose of Honor

use and development of the concept of *honra*, the single most important theme he undertakes for his plays, and a formula that will find its way into the dramas of his contemporaries and his epigones, Calderón's particularly. I could not hope to exhaust the theme of *honra* in this chapter. It is my purpose to show how it is perceived both by the public and by other writers, in this case principally by Cervantes. My interest is to show how Cervantes's own literary production in *Las novelas ejemplares* offers a human and professional literary response to the use of the theme in the *comedia* and his personal reactions to some of the socially acceptable uses of *honra*.

It was well known in the social ideology of the time that Jews and Moors could not have *honra*. Perhaps part of this negative disposition toward Jews was the idea that they were traitors of Christ. Frederick R. Bryson notes:

> Another class excluded from the possession of honor, Torelli added, are Jews. He held that as heretics are traitors to the Church, so Jews are traitors to their king, who is Christ.... Benavides said that they are base, infamous, and without honor; that, like the pygmies, they are fit to fight only with cranes; that the death of Christ has made them the Christians' prisoners and slaves; and that, being obstinate and treacherous usurers who are always sinning by their cruel methods of making money, they are a brood of vipers. (26)

Américo Castro stresses the importance of the theme in the dramatic genre: "La estructura y el ideal castizo de la vida española fueron, por tanto, los motivos de haber sido llevados a la escena los temas de honra, las venganzas atroces" ("El drama de la honra" 40). He also notes, with respect to the theme of "limpieza de sangre," "Los dramas de honra tenían como invisible trasfondo el drama vivo de los estatutos de limpieza de sangre, y las prolongadas polémicas acerca de su conveniencia o inconveniencia" (45). Van Beysterveldt also emphasizes the link in the theater between literature and the concept of *limpieza* (5). He believes that the actions of some of the characters are a result of the abuses of the statutes of *pureté de sang* (192). Van Beysterveldt points to an interesting idea of that time:

> Il y a entre les auteurs dramatiques du Siècle d'or comme une conspiration du silence sur le conflit qui déchirait l'Espagne

Chapter Four

> selon les témoignages irrécusables des statuts de pureté de sang, un conflit dont l'apogée tragique coïncide précisément avec le triomphe de la comedia. (184)

Alongside this "conspiration du silence," Van Beysterveldt notes the use of techniques such as "double sens" in which to couch some of the preoccupations brought about by statutes of *pureté de sang.* (See p. 98. See also Peristiany 9–18; Caro Baroja, "Honour and Shame"; and Larson.)

It is inconceivable that one could think of the major plays without the use of the *honra* principle as a generating force, or of Lope's plays without *honra* as an identifying marker. The presentation of the theme in a dramatic setting had the effect of reinforcing the public's own basic belief in the efficacy of such a concept as a way of life. However, dramatists like Lope and others had to smooth over some of the edges and contours of the practice so that what one sees on the stage is in some ways what Van Beysterveldt describes as "une image idéalisée de la réalité, où rien n'était possible sans la complicité de 'l'opinion'" (25). To indicate something good and outstanding, people in the seventeenth century said "Es de Lope." How was Cervantes affected by Lope's popularity? What were his true feelings about Lope as dramatist? What was his understanding of the *honra* principle as a human device and as a technique or dramatic principle? These are some of the questions I hope to answer in the course of this chapter. Basically, I suggest that Cervantes had a negative or critical stance toward Lope, caused in part by Lope's success as a dramatist and his own as a "failed" dramatist within the canon of the *comedia* (a grouping determined largely by Lope and his world). The four stories I analyze below represent Cervantes's response to *honra* as a concept of life and as a topos of literature.

I
"La fuerza de la sangre"

The basic plot of "La fuerza de la sangre" can easily be identified with common actions, events, and themes of drama. An arrogant young man, Rodolfo, conceives a passion for Leocadia, whom he meets accidentally while cavorting with friends. Her father reproves Rodolfo and his friends for their unseemly

The Prose of Honor

conduct. Rodolfo arranges to kidnap Leocadia, whom he takes to his room, and there rapes her. She is in effect "dishonored" by Rodolfo by losing her virginity to him, even under these terrible circumstances. She is caught unaware at first, but later when Rodolfo wishes to continue taking his pleasure, she thwarts him. After she takes note of some features of the room she is in, Rodolfo leads her to the street and lets her return home. She and her parents are aware that she has been dishonored, but her father's relatively lowly status does not enable him to take the accustomed vengeance immediately, easily, or at all. Rodolfo, after all, is the child of rich parents. As a result of his violation of her, Leocadia becomes pregnant and gives birth to a beautiful male child, who is raised by her and her parents. In a street incident the child is trampled by a horse. Through coincidental circumstances (a literary manipulation by Cervantes, probably following the Byzantine romance tradition), the injured child is brought to the house of Rodolfo's parents, who do not know that this is Rodolfo's son. Leocadia, however, begins to recognize the room as the one in which she lost her honor. After inquiring discreetly, she realizes that it is indeed Rodolfo's house (Rodolfo has since left for Italy and is in Naples). Leocadia reveals her problem to Rodolfo's mother, Estefanía, who, because of sympathy for Leocadia's dilemma (as a reflection of the code of *honra*) and affection for the child, conceives of a ruse to lure Rodolfo back to fulfill his moral obligations to Leocadia and the child. Rodolfo is tricked by the women, and in a surprise gesture, Leocadia is brought in. They recognize each other. A priest is called, who later performs their marriage, and the original order that has been violated is restored. The couple lives on and has an illustrious life in Toledo.

The usual basic situation would have been for someone to avenge Leocadia's dishonor immediately or as soon as possible in order to provide her with the proper personal and social response. According to the conventional formula concerning *honra*, Rodolfo would either marry her or meet his end for what he did. That the text is a treatment of *honra* is reinforced by the various allusions to it. Her parents are wary about turning to the authorities after she is kidnapped because they are "confusos, sin saber si sería bien dar noticia de su desgracia a

Chapter Four

la justicia, temerosos no fuesen ellos el principal instrumento de publicar su deshonra" (2: 78). This reluctance to make public an incident that might mark Leocadia socially is repeated when she says, "—pues es mejor la deshonra que se ignora que la honra que está puesta en opinión de las gentes" (2: 79).[1] Leocadia's despair is evidenced when she tells Rodolfo she has lost "la mejor prenda" (2: 79) against her will and declares: "—¡Quítamela [la vida] al momento, que no es bien que la tenga la que no tiene honra!" (2: 79).[2] Her father charts out an equation that relieves Leocadia when he makes a distinction between sin and virtue: "—la verdadera deshonra está en el pecado y la verdadera honra en la virtud" (2: 84). In this way, her father is showing that the sin is the responsibility of Rodolfo, who raped his daughter and who acted in a dishonorable fashion, while Leocadia's innocence and reluctance to give in to his advances clearly labels her as an honorable person who was wronged: Rodolfo is the sinner and Leocadia the virtuous one. This leads to a consideration of public virtue as opposed to private virtue.[3] In the social and public view, Leocadia is dishonored and must live with the social consequences of her dishonor in spite of her innocence. Her inner virtue is affirmed by the narrator and by her own soliloquy describing her valiant fight to ward off her unwanted lover. She, therefore, clearly is presented as a virtuous person unjustly violated. Cervantes takes great pains to prevent his heroine from falling to the social level of tainted woman.

Estefanía, the rapist's mother, seeks to ascertain the truth of Leocadia's story by having her son's friends admit to the adventure. Her motive works well with the second part of the *honra* equation (*honra/virtud*): "porque el saber la verdad desto importaba la honra y el sosiego de todos sus parientes" (2: 90).

The thematic core of the tale is the lost honor of Leocadia, but the Cervantine approach is to associate it not with the conventional treatment of lost honor—social marginalization—but rather with a sound and reasonable understanding that is not prejudicial to Leocadia's honor.[4] The dénouement—the arrival of Rodolfo and the anagnorisis—restores Leocadia's *virtud* in a social context. Her marriage forgives and exonerates Rodolfo, who is shamed into accepting his responsibility. Cervantes, in effect, is offering us a tale in which no one is left punished; no

The Prose of Honor

one is killed as is expected in the social *honra* case. He offers us an artistic and social solution to a flagrant abuse by humanizing the end.[5]

There is yet another feature of the tale that may point to Cervantes's theatrical sensitivity. I refer to the presence of space as it is used in the *novela*. It goes beyond mere utilization as a mimetic support.

The reader becomes aware of space early in the story because the action begins in the public plaza. The family of Leocadia comes upon a group of young rowdies carrying on. The next scenario is Rodolfo's house and room. This is extremely important because Rodolfo has tried to deceive Leocadia as to where she is. Her awareness of details in the room presages her recognition of who precisely her assailant was. This use of space, here in the room, is tied to a perception of visibility and gives the picture of a stage with multiple planes and levels.

There is considerable reason for seeing dramatic effects in a short story. Marina S. Brownlee points to the "novela comediesca," which is strongly linked to dramatic devices (21). She also notes, with respect to "La prudente venganza," "that a fluid relationship exists between the novella and *comedia* genres and that a rigid set of generic distinctions and prescriptive rules is of no real value" (23). Her repetition of Othón Arróniz's remarks concerning the similarity to drama apparent in Lope's *Novelas a Marcia Leonarda* must be applied also to Cervantes, whose *novelas* also have this feature as intrinsic elements in and of themselves. Lope's awareness of the generic proximity between the drama and the short story is particularly important here, and such a link may have easily been seen earlier by Cervantes. It is not idle to say that the *Novelas a Marcia Leonarda* were largely inspired by Cervantes's collection. Lope says: " 'tienen las novelas los mismos preceptos que las comedias, cuyo fin es haber dado su autor contento y gusto al pueblo, aunque se ahorque el arte; y esto, aunque va dicho al descuido, fue opinión de Aristóteles' " (cited by Brownlee 14). Menéndez Pidal perceptively focuses on particular features of the *novela* as opposed to drama:

> pero a la vez creo que esa discrepancia depende también del distinto género literario en que el conflicto se desarrolla.

Chapter Four

> La novela destinada a la lectura privada invitaba a la reflexión condenatoria de una venganza sangrienta, mientras el teatro exigía entregarse a los sentimientos de mayor efectismo" ("Del honor" 170)

There was a flexibility of adopting and adapting genres (see Tómov 623). That this dramatic feature of *Las novelas ejemplares* was obvious to Cervantes's contemporaries is to be ascertained in Avellaneda, about whom Francisco Rico says, "Curiosamente, el responsable del *Don Quijote* apócrifo, Alonso Fernández de Avellaneda, tachaba a las *Novelas ejemplares* de 'comedias en prosa': obras ayunas, pues, de transcendencia artística, mero pasatiempo" (11). Maria Elisa Ciavarelli, among others, has noted that the use of the female *disfraz* is very much a dramatic device in the short story setting (see 188–89): "tema de la mujer disfrazada de hombre [which I treat later in "Las dos doncellas"] en busca de su amante, tan popular en la novelística y teatro renacentistas, frecuentemente encontrado en Cervantes, entremezclado al tema de la honra y al de la fuerza de la sangre" (questions of genre are perceptively discussed by Rosalie Colie, *The Resources of Kind*).

Further dramatic possiblities are seen in Leocadia's lament. Her dialogue (and in some cases her soliloquy) is reminiscent of dramatic production. Her soliloquy is used in a dramatically functional way because she wishes to share her innermost thoughts on her situation, not necessarily with Rodolfo but more with the public. In the final analysis, the public is her judge within the social view of integrity and *honra*.[6]

After the heinous rape, Rodolfo brings Leocadia back to the plaza, hoping that she will not be able to recognize him or where she was. But Cervantes adds a detail that is dramatic in character. Rodolfo mumbles some words in a "voz trocada y en lengua medio portuguesa" (2: 82). This vocality is reminiscent of certain dramatic typologies and characterizations (cf. Quevedo in his *Buscón*). Also the purpose is strictly auditory and not predominantly *lisible*. The vocality of other aspects of the defense that Leocadia makes to her parents elicits from her father the qualification of "tu discreto *discurso* [emphasis mine]." Orality is the second dimension to the reader's expectation.

The scene changes from Leocadia's house to the public square where her son is injured and returns again to Rodolfo's house.

The Prose of Honor

There another important feature of orality is manifested. Leocadia shares her words with Estefanía. It is a type of confession, the kind that occurs between parents or lovers (see also the conversation between Estefanía and Rodolfo [2: 90–91]). It is an intense moment because it is the only time Leocadia reveals her secret (outside of the immediate family circle). This is a form of dramatic intimacy that Cervantes explores and exploits; it is in very many ways a dramaturgical device.

The dénouement makes greater sense if viewed as a dramatic manipulation within a prose context. Estefanía joins Leocadia in her grand design, first glimpsed with the purloining of the crucifix, regarded as a witness (a visible datum). She insists that Rodolfo's friends be present, thereby ironically reversing the notion of social pressure—his judges will now be the same people who assisted him in the kidnapping of Leocadia. Together, they view his uneasiness when faced with the pseudo *retrato* as he declines the marriage offer on grounds that the anonymous candidate does not meet his expectations of beauty. Estefanía and Leocadia's plot is aimed at forcing Rodolfo to undo his sin by marrying Leocadia. As a "tainted" woman, and a woman from a lesser social class and economic situation, this forcing is rather extreme. Estefanía (with the assent of her husband) does not stand on the social custom of avoiding people of different social stations. Rodolfo will be made to acknowledge his responsibility and be forced to resolve the tainted situation by marrying Leocadia.

The final scene with the fainting of Leocadia, the seeming fainting state of Rodolfo, the arrival of the priest who presumably will render final rites and extreme unction to the apparently dead Leocadia, all add to a group picture particularly meaningful in its visual power. Even the final outcome, the wedding, *cum* wedding party and dinner, is accented as visible and dramatic. Prose has been molded and crafted by a principle of visibility and dramatic action, conceived, I am sure, as an alternative to genre as well as an alternative to morality and social conduct.

The historicity of this tale is to be found in the preponderant place that the theme of honor occupies in Spanish life. In fact, what we term "la vida española" would be incomplete without an acknowledgment of its presence therein. Its place,

Chapter Four

therefore, in this *novela* is Cervantes's recognition of the ubiquity of the theme in Spanish life.

II
"La señora Cornelia"

The historical markers of "La señora Cornelia" naturally accommodate the theme of *honra,* although with a touch of parody. That there is a dramaturgical sensitivity to the work is corroborated by these words, spoken by one of the characters when contemplating the development of the conflict of the story: "—¿Qué ha de ser . . . sino que yo quiero hacer un personaje en esta trágica comedia?" (2: 267). The development of the story does in fact remind the reader of a drama based on the question of *honra,* which comes very close to a Lopean play. The reader is put on alert at the beginning of the story when Don Juan, one of two Spanish noblemen who are studying in the city, while walking the dark streets of Bologna, has a newborn child thrust into his arms. When a voice asks him if he is Fabio, Don Juan answers affirmatively and takes the child, whom he brings to his rooms. The next scene involves a street fracas with sword play in which one of the participants says, "—Mientes, que aquí no hay ningún traidor; que el querer cobrar la honra perdida, a toda demasía da licencia" (2: 245). The Spaniard renders assistance to the fallen man.

A young woman, Señora Cornelia, reveals her dilemma to the Spaniards. She and her brother were orphans, but her brother complied with his social responsibility in looking out for her honor ("—en poder de mi hermano, el cual desde niña puso en mi guarda al recato mismo, puesto que más confiaba de mi honrada condición que de la solicitud que ponía en guardarme" (2: 252).[7] In spite of her brother's vigilance, Cornelia falls in love with the Duke of Ferrara. She gives herself to him, but she insists—and in a detail that is crucial for Cervantine resolutions to problems of lost honor (cf. Dorotea in *Don Quijote,* part 1)—under the promise that he would marry her; she later discovers she is pregnant. The street fracas was the encounter between the Duke and her brother and his friends, who went to settle accounts. The emotion of the situation causes her to give birth that night.

The Prose of Honor

Her brother Lorenzo discusses the matter with Don Juan. Lorenzo describes his role in Cornelia's life: "—Ser yo honrado y ella muchacha y hermosa me hacían andar solícito en guardarla; pero todas mis prevenciones y diligencias las ha defraudado la voluntad arrojada de mi hermana Cornelia . . ." (2: 257). In his talk Lorenzo gives us details that neither Cornelia nor the Duke gives us. Lorenzo ends by saying, "—yo me veo sin hermana y sin honra" (2: 257); the conventional status of a dishonored person is not confined solely to Cornelia, who lost her honor to the Duke while being unmarried. It therefore behooves Lorenzo to take action to defend his own lost honor. Lorenzo says further:

> —puesto que todo esto hasta agora por mi parte lo tengo puesto debajo de la llave del silencio, y no he querido contar a nadie este agravio hasta ver si le puedo remediar y satisfacer en alguna manera. . . . (2: 257)

The social code insists that a male member of the family confront the offender and obtain satisfaction:

> —que las infamias mejor es que se presuman y sospechen que no que se sepan de cierto y distintamente, que entre el sí y el no de la duda cada uno puede inclinarse a la parte que más quisiere, y cada una tendrá sus valedores. Finalmente, yo tengo determinado de ir a Ferrara y pedir al mismo duque la satisfac[c]ión de mi ofensa, y si la negare, desafiarle sobre el caso. . . . (2: 257–58)

Lorenzo's role in this matter is clearly defined by social (and in this case literary) mores, and he will act accordingly. He will face the offender of his sister's and his own honor squarely ("de persona a persona" [2: 258]). As part of the narrative design, the reader is justified in preparing him/herself. The encounter between the aggrieved brother and the offending Duke gives a clue, I believe, to the quality of Cervantes's treatment of the honor theme here. The reader/spectator is justified in expecting fireworks but is somewhat let down when the two meet and the offending lover proves to be somewhat "mild." He rejects any claim that he dishonored anyone. Whatever he did to Cornelia was done under his promise as her "esposo," therefore

Chapter Four

there is no violation of the code. But why has the Duke not made good on his promise? His mother wants him to marry Livia! The potentially explosive situation never materializes; it is a tempest in a teapot. Even the fracas in retrospect was unnecessary. When the Duke gives his reason for not yet marrying Cornelia the potential for dramatic action is deflated, and all the previous and present claims about living without honor or defending one's honor come close to farce. Don Juan's question in a way indirectly reveals his crestfallen expectations: "—De modo, señor—dijo don Juan—, [que] cuando Cornelia y vuestro hijo pareciesen ¿no negaréis ser vuestra esposa y él vuestro hijo?" (2: 266). Further farcical dimensions appear, as in the confrontation between the Duke and Lorenzo, who under "normal" conditions should be quite antagonistic to each other: "Adelantóse el duque a recebirle con los brazos abiertos, y la primera palabra que le dijo fue llamarle hermano" (2: 266). A further comic dimension is achieved when we read, "A esto respondió el señor Lorenzo arrojándose a los pies del duque, que porfiaba por levantarlo" (2: 267). The dimensions of a plot along the lines of "All's well that ends well" is underscored by Lorenzo, who says:

> —De vuestra cristiandad y grandeza, serenísimo señor y hermano mío, no podíamos mi hermana y yo esperar menor bien del que a entrambos nos hacéis: a ella, en igualarla con vos, y a mí, en ponerme en el número de vuestro. (2: 267)

It is noteworthy that Lorenzo should use the term *cristiandad,* underscoring that the Duke's solution to the problem is of a Christian nature. Américo Castro's view here is urgently important: "Frente a tal desdicha, Cervantes pensaba que la solución razonable—y, en último término, la única cristiana—era olvidar a la mujer, dejarla ir e impedirle el retorno: 'a enemigo que huye.'. . . Pero Cervantes tenía propias ideas acerca de las 'opiniones' de sus compatriotas" ("El drama de la honra" 35); he further notes: "O sea, que por debajo de ser villano o caballero, cristiano viejo o nuevo, yace el proceder como cristiano interiormente, una idea que a Cervantes le venía de su trato con erasmistas" ("El drama de la honra" 219–20). See also Van Beysterveldt who, quoting Fray Gerónimo, says:

> "Mais ni la charité chrétienne ni les statuts eux-mêmes n'autorisent à perpétuer à l'infini ce déshonneur," fait remarquer Fray Gerónimo. Et il poursuit: "Qui peut nier qu'on fait tort à une famille quand, après qu'elle a joui pendant des générations des honneurs qui reviennent aux Chrétiens fidèles, on répand en public le sang de son honneur sous prétexte de servir le droit et la religion, et qu'on lui fait subir ce qui peut être considéré comme une 'mort civile'?" Le texte [of his *Defensa de los estatutos y noblezas españolas*] dit: "... y con una *muerte ciuil* [Van Beysterveldt's emphasis], queda apartado de los demás viuientes, y se descubre el pecado que ha dozientos años estuuo encubierto en la tierra." (5)

Domingo Ricart observes this theme in Cervantes: "La ética de Cervantes es, por tanto, menos instintiva que la reflejada en el teatro, *más cristiana* [emphasis mine]; es, en suma, erasmiana, dispuesta al perdón y a la resignación ante el fracaso y la ofensa, en vez de recurrir a la solución salvaje de la venganza para defender la propia dignidad" (53). Menéndez Pidal also focuses on Cervantes (and others) as following an "ética individualista" ("Del honor" 177).

It should be noted that there is an account of another feature associated with questions of honor and sexist exploitation. Cornelia says:

> —Mil veces le dije que públicamente me pidiese a mi hermano, pues no era posible que me negase, y que no había que dar disculpas al vulgo de la culpa que le pondrían de la desigualdad de nuestro casamiento, pues no desmentía en nada la nobleza del linaje Bentibolli a la suya Estense. (2: 252)

Her brother sees the problem differently, which may account in some way for his wholehearted reception of the Duke on more pacific and less violent terms. Lorenzo says:

> —Hame dicho mi parienta, que es la que todo esto me ha dicho, que el duque engañó a mi hermana debajo de palabra de recebirla por mujer. Esto yo no lo creo, por ser desigual el matrimonio en cuanto a los bienes de fortuna, que en los de naturaleza el mundo sabe la calidad de los Bentibollis de Bolonia. (2: 257)

Chapter Four

The comedy continues when the narrator describes the unlikely moment of joining between the offender and the offended: "—Ya en esto se le arrasaban los ojos de lágrimas, y al duque lo mismo, enternecidos, el uno con la pérdida de su esposa, y el otro, con el hallazgo de tan buen cuñado" (2: 267). It is then that Don Antonio (the other Spaniard) elucidates the clear intention of the author—to "prosify" a normally dramatic situation—by calling himself a "personaje" in this "trágica comedia" (2: 267). The word *trágica* can only be looked upon as out of place, since the first stage of a "happy ending" has just been completed (peace between the Duke and the aggrieved brother).

A lingering touch of the social norm of keeping potentially damaging *honra* situations hidden appears when the parties realize that the Duke's intentions will be proved when Cornelia is confronted with him:

> Con esto se consolaron todos, y no quisieron hacer la inquisición de buscalla por bandos públicos, sino por diligencias secretas, pues de nadie sino de su prima se sabía su falta; y entre los que no sabían la intención del duque correría riesgo el crédito de su hermana si la pregonasen, y ser gran trabajo andar satisfaciendo a cada uno de las sospechas que una vehemente presunción les infunde. (2: 271)

The final step is the actual meeting between the "dishonored" Cornelia and the Duke: "y así en silencio honesto y amoroso se gozaban los dos felices amantes y esposos verdaderos" (2: 274). Cervantes creates a momentary obstacle by having the Duke play an ill-advised joke on his brother-in-law. Once they marry and the Duke's mother conveniently dies, the *lutos* are changed into *galas,* a festive scene ensues, and just as in the conventional *comedia,* the confidants Sulpicia and Fabio also marry, balancing off the picture.

It is not difficult to decipher Cervantes's point of view as author from the general lines of the play. The story goes from a dramatic encounter of initial violence, to the admission and revelation of Cornelia's dishonor, to the brother's intention of responding to the code of honor by seeking satisfaction from her offender, then, on to the very peaceful resolution of the honor/dishonor situation with marriage legitimizing the passion between the two lovers (and the conventional removal of the obstacle to happiness in the person of the Duke's mother). As in "La fuerza de la sangre," Cervantes rejects the convention of a violent resolution involving the death(s) of the characters involved. He is saying, as it were, that a far more satisfying and less violent and hence more rational resolution is achieved through the marriage of the two principals. Cervantes takes the conventional *comedia,* re-frames it as prose, and deflates its means and intentions in favor of humane, rational, and Christian resolutions. This he does by contriving to metamorphose the original tragic situation to a semicomical, almost farcical one. Clearly, Cervantes's rejection of "bloody *honra*" must be read as a form of antihonor in "La señora Cornelia."

III
"Las dos doncellas"

"Las dos doncellas" also treats the myth of *honra,* but perhaps in a more serious manner than the previously discussed story. In it Teodosia is deceived by Marco Antonio, who enjoys her sexual favors under the unofficial title of *esposo.* Teodosia, dressed as a man, runs away and spends the night at an inn. Another traveler shares the room with her, and unknown to them both it is her brother Rafael. After a series of experiences, the brother and sister, who are looking for Marco Antonio, come upon a beautiful young man who turns out to be Leocadia, a rich woman who also fell in love with Marco Antonio. She granted him an assignation, but at the last minute he did not appear. She, too, is searching for Marco Antonio. They all come upon him, and during a pitched battle Marco Antonio is wounded. Seeing Leocadia, he confesses that in reality he first became *comprometido* to Teodosia; therefore, he rightfully is obligated to fulfill his promise to her. Rafael, Teodosia's brother, is in love with Leocadia. All agree to marry, and on the return home they witness a battle between two knights, who turn out to be the fathers of Teodosia and Leocadia, against the father of Marco Antonio, whom they accuse of having known of the son's deception.

In this tale there is a double question of honor: both women have a claim on Marco Antonio's promise of marriage. Teodosia's case is strengthened by the fact that she has a brother whose responsibility it is to defend their honor, since her lost

111

Chapter Four

honor bequeaths to him and their father the moral responsibility of saving her. The reader must question why Cervantes has two women with the same complaint. The answer, I believe, resides in the need for telling a suspenseful story. The double complication here must lead to something drastic, and the reader's attention is held until fairly late in the tale, when Marco Antonio clarifies the priorities of his moral obligations. The reader has stayed with the presumptions of the tale long enough to have been told a good story. Marco Antonio falls back on subtle but important distinctions, and Cervantes solves the second half of the *queja* motif by having Rafael marry Leocadia, a solution as practical in prose as it is in drama. That the principle of *honra* extends to the relatives of the dishonored person is further demonstrated by Cervantes's having the two aggrieved fathers battle Marco Antonio's father.

The double dishonor motif can be seen as Cervantes's going Lope one better—not one dishonored person but two—and once again in the resolution, although it comes dangerously close to violence (the confrontation between the respective fathers), Cervantes opts for the pacific, nonviolent alternative, implying that "casos de honra" do not need to be solved by spilling blood. Cervantes's human response comes to the fore once again, as in "La señora Cornelia" and "La fuerza de la sangre."[8]

Previously I suggested that in response to dramatic convention, Cervantes parodies some of the conventional posturing of dishonored lovers. The ill and recovering Marco Antonio (casuistically) explaining to Leocadia that Teodosia has precedence over her in his love is a form of (subtle) humor, if not parody of legal and theological discourse. If Cervantes is not parodying *honra* situations as they appear in the theater, he certainly is manipulating the action for the sake of entertainment.

As in the previous story, where we examined the role of the brother vis-à-vis the resolution of the honor conflict, here, too, Cervantes manipulates and perhaps trivializes some features of the dénouement when he has Rafael, Teodosia's brother, say to Marco Antonio:

> —Volved en vos, señor mío, y abrazad a vuestro amigo y a vuestro hermano, pues vos queréis que lo sea. Conoced a don Rafael, vuestro camarada, que será el verdadero testigo

The Prose of Honor

de vuestra voluntad y de la merced que a su hermana queréis hacer con admitirla por vuestra. (2: 229)

His sudden friendship is justified inasmuch as Marco Antonio's confession, which prepares the way for the marriage that would solve the "yerros de amor," sounds a bit tinny. The kind of bravura, force, and strength normally expected of a brother or father in such a circumstance is simply not there. The coincidence of the two fathers doing their part to avenge the respective dishonors of their daughters seems like a last ditch effort by Cervantes to revive in the minds of his readers that old conventional bloody resolution. In a true tragic case of an *honra* violation, he might have had one or both of the fathers killed, not knowing that all infractions on their daughter's honor have been amended (a solution somewhat closer to Italianate stories). The fact that supporters and defenders of the fathers break into applause when they see the fathers embracing ("Todos fueron a abrazar a los peregrinos con muestras de contento tales que no se pueden encarecer" [2: 236]) echoes the author's own reservations about bloody resolutions. The last gesture is exhausted—and in a happy way—leaving the readers with a nonconventional resolution of lost *honra* lingering in their minds and the belief of "All's well that ends well" as the author's final say on the matter.

IV
"El celoso extremeño"

I have saved for last the best and perhaps the most significant example of Cervantes's treatment of a case of *honra* in his *Novelas ejemplares*, "El celoso extremeño."[9] It is here that Cervantes creates a situation that is unmistakable, leaves no room for humor or parody, and supplements the conventional views of the honor question. In this tale all of the social and literary features are brought together.

From the very beginning Cervantes structures a situation that puts the reader on alert. He creates a situation in which a man (Carrizales) advanced in years (approximately 68) marries a very young woman, 13 or 14 years old, from a family of limited means. The older man returns to Spain as a rich *perulero*.[10]

113

Chapter Four

The element that threatens the domestic situation is the Extremaduran's pathological jealousy. To underscore this situation, Cervantes reverts to caricature in describing the extent of the old man's mania. Carrizales puts Leonora (his young wife) in a separate part of the house;[11] he will not allow any male animals in the house; he will not allow tailors to fit his wife directly. The obvious reason for this is to create the groundwork for a particular kind of dénouement, which will show that Leonora was placed in a situation of extreme circumstances, and that her conduct could be excused, or, at least, understood.

Loaysa, a sensual young man, serves as the serpent in this garden of Eden. He realizes that something of value is concealed in that house and is determined to find out what it is. In order to gain entrance to the sacred quarter of the house, he manages to trick the black eunuch who lives in Carrizales's house. He gets into the confidence first of the white slaves and then of a duenna that Carrizales, the jealous husband, has employed.

The extreme difference in age between Carrizales and his wife should give the first indication that we shall be dealing with the question of *honra*. Cervantes obviously has decided to treat the theme in stages; for illustrative purposes one can visualize a series of concentric circles. The outermost circle is represented by the black eunuch and the servants/slaves who, against all the rules of the house, admit Loaysa to hear him play music. This is the first stage of betrayal.

The second circle is the stratagem used to allow the household members and Leonora to enjoy fully the company of Loaysa. This consists of putting a sleeping draught in Carrizales's wine. The effect of this draught is to ensure that Carrizales will sleep through anything. At these early stages, in a manner reminiscent of dramatic pieces of the Golden Age, the narrator brings up the question of *honra*. He says:

> A este contradijo su señora con muchas veras, diciendo que no se hiciese la tal cosa ni la tal entrada, porque le pesaría en el alma [to let Loaysa directly into the house], pues desde allí le podían ver y oír a su salvo y sin peligro de su [Leonora's] honra. (2: 118)

The duenna answers haughtily and incautiously:

The Prose of Honor

> —¿Qué honra?—dijo la dueña—. El Rey tiene harta.[12] Estése vuesa merced encerrada con su Metusalén, y déjenos a nosotras holgar como pudiéremos. (2: 118)

The impetus toward a violation of the honor code with dramatic possibilities seems to be moving forward, since allowing Loaysa to enter the house carries with it the express possibility that Carrizales might awaken.

The next step is proposed and represents an *astucia* used to gain entrance into the sacred and secret part of the house. Loaysa wants to make a wax impression of the key in order to make another key with which to get near Leonora.

In the next, and clearly the most substantial violation of the honor code, Leonora herself agrees to anoint her husband's wrists and nostrils with a special ointment that will have the desired effect of keeping him soundly asleep. In effect, Leonora betrays the unstated but well-known hope that Carrizales (and society) had for such situations. His beloved becomes his mortal enemy. Yet another feature of Leonora's fall from fortune operates at a basic level of sensuality. She lived with Carrizales in a marital state for a short time, and now Loaysa comes into play as an object of love and lust. The reader is informed that while the other members of the household are praising the physical traits of Loaysa, Leonora, in whom the currents of feeling and lust are moving, also becomes aware of him: "Sola Leonora callaba, y le miraba, y le iba pareciendo de mejor talle que su velado" (2: 125). It is an important detail also for the ending. Having implicated herself in the betrayal of Carrizales's wishes, she now "sins" in her mind; which, given the honor code of the time, even in its narrowest application, is a serious breach.

The next concentric circle of honor violation is the actual fall of Leonora through the exhortations of the duenna. The narrator states:

> En fin, tanto dijo la dueña, tanto persuadió la dueña, que Leonora se rindió, Leonora se engañó y Leonora se perdió, dando en tierra con todas las prevenciones del discreto Carrizales, que *dormía el sueño de la muerte de su honra* [emphasis mine]. (2: 129)

The wall that Carrizales had built comes tumbling down. The narrator describes it: "¡Todo aqueso derribó por los fundamentos

Chapter Four

la astucia . . . !" (2: 129). The *astucia* that Loaysa uses is in every sense a picaresque (read "prose") device. Symbolically, one can read how the prose device tears down the dramatic one; or put another way, prose can deal with an honor question every bit as well as can drama. The end of Leonora's virtue and honor is also the end of the generic propriety of drama to deal with *casos de honra,* and no one can deny the skill and artistic success of this story.

Another stage of the violation of the question of *honra* begins when Carrizales unexpectedly awakens and sees his bride in the arms of Loaysa: Carrizales "pensó perder el juicio. . . . Vió a Leonora en brazos de Loaysa, durmiendo tan a sueño suelto como si en ellos obrara la virtud del ungüento y no en el celoso anciano" (2: 130). In a number of instances Américo Castro points to a scenario that is played out before us in this case. The situation in which Carrizales finds himself here is already preordained in terms of its solution and resolution: "matar a la adúltera, real o supuesta" (Américo Castro, "El drama de la honra" 17; see also 34 for a discussion of the links with *cristiano nuevo/cristiano viejo* complications). Given the fact that later there will be a qualification as to whether Leonora has or has not given herself to Loaysa, it is important to recall that whether she did or did not, given the contemporary *honra/opinión* binomial, she is as good as guilty: " 'Carlos de Paomar mató a María Samper, su mujer, porque le dijeron que era adúltera, sin haberla hallado con hombre' " (Américo Castro, "El drama de la honra" 40). Castro also points to Lope's *La esclava de su galán,* " 'un hombre tan airado, / que mató mal informado, / su desdichada mujer' " ("El drama de la honra" 107n17bis). It is particularly ironic that Lope supposedly claims that bloody solutions are not to his pleasure (Menéndez Pidal, "Del honor" 171). Whether Lope liked such solutions or not, this was the expected resolution to "casos de honra." Then it would mean that if Cervantes were not censuring Lope, he was certainly censuring the whole concept of the *comedia* that Lope's dramaturgy with its accent on "casos de honra porque mueven con fuerza a toda gente" gave. Given the readers' expectations in this situation, George Northup voices his repugnance at the barbarity of a situation in which mere suspicions and not facts would be enough to condemn a person to death. Sympathy is accorded to the aggrieved husband but none to the wife (xxi).

The Prose of Honor

The natural expectation is for the aggrieved husband to kill both lovers. Here Cervantes cleverly and cagily puts Carrizales one step away from the final situation; in a sense he is buying himself time in order to carry out the solution he prefers.

> Y, con todo eso, tomara la venganza que aquella grande maldad requería si se hallara con armas para poder tomarla;[13] y así, determinó volverse a su aposento a tomar una daga, y volver a sacar las manchas de su honra con sangre de sus dos enemigos. . . . (2: 130)

Having a dangerous weapon at hand meant that Carrizales would satisfy the conventional honor code by killing his wife and her lover. Another detail will acknowledge another facet of the honor code—the implications and consequences of a violation of *honra* as they affect one's family. Carrizales orders that Leonora's parents be brought to the house, but the *deus ex machina* here is the faint (or stroke) that Carrizales suffers. His serious illness incapacitates him and will prevent the execution of the final dictates of the honor code. Here the reader sees another facet of Leonora when she is described as "abrazándose con su esposo, le hacía las mayores caricias que jamás le habría hecho" (2: 131). Américo Castro has commented on the two endings of this story (see "El celoso extremeño de Cervantes"). Perhaps one kind of reader might have wanted Leonora to have been caught *in flagrante* (as in the case of Mateo Alemán's Dorida and Bonifacio). This certainly would have left nothing in doubt. However, the final ending is effective even if Cervantes emphasizes the nonsexual aspect of the meeting. Carrizales saw Leonora *in the arms of Loaysa* (emphasis mine). Such an encounter even without explicit sexuality was equal in effect to his having found them in the middle of lovemaking. The punishment for either case would be the same.

It is at this point that Cervantes overturns the expected solution. This is in part prepared for by the fact of Carrizales's physical inability to carry on. In the final dénouement one sees what Cervantes really thinks of the honor code. Carrizales says:

> La venganza que pienso tomar desta afrenta no es ni ha de ser de las que ordinariamente suelen tomarse, pues quiero que, así como yo fui estremado en lo que hice, así sea la venganza que tomaré, tomándola de mí mismo como del más

Chapter Four

> culpado en este delito. . . . Yo fui el que, como el gusano de seda, me fabriqué la casa donde muriese, y a ti no te culpo, ¡oh niña mal aconsejada!—y diciendo esto se inclinó y besó el rostro de la desmayada Leonora. . . . (2: 133)[14]

In addition to not murdering the two who destroyed his own honor, he suggests that Leonora *marry* her lover, seeing perhaps that his union with her was unstable and unfortunate from the very beginning. Cervantes, therefore, opts not for the bloody resolution, but in a manner reminiscent of Moratín a century later, has Carrizales rationally acknowledge his failing and guilt in the matter (which also acknowledges the role that his pathological case of jealousy, so odd and even humorous at the beginning of the story, had in causing the supposed adultery). More than Carrizales's rationality, it is Cervantes's humanity that brings about the resolution of this case. There is no vengeance as in many a dramatic spectacle but sadness (which acknowledges the fall as a sad one in human terms) and sorrow. This is the extent to which Carrizales will go while not murdering his spouse and her lover. His humanity is further seen in one of his last acts toward his wife: "Hizo Carrizales su testamento en la manera que había dicho, sin declarar el yerro de Leonora . . ." (2: 134). There is always the possiblity that the case might become known publicly, but to make an effort at protecting Leonora's good name, he deliberately does not mention her *yerro* in his will. Leonora repeats her defense to Carrizales: "sabed que no os he ofendido sino con el pensamiento" (2: 134). At this stage her statement really has no effect because, as stated above, in the honor code, being found in the arms of another person is the same as having given him her body. The final detail of the story has Leonora becoming a nun. How ironic and how Cervantine it is that after spending many years in the New World, Carrizales returns wealthy as Croesus, yet all of this wealth will never be enjoyed by his descendants. When Leonora decides to take vows as a nun, her goods, wealth, i.e., her dowry, and the estate that Carrizales leaves to her, conventionally would go to the order that she joins.

This story as a product of a deconstruction of a genre—the honor code dramas—may well be the best tale of the collection and is the strongest statement that Cervantes makes about *honra* both in life and in art.

The Prose of Honor

In sum, Cervantes rejects the common social and literary response to a violation of the code of honor that would be mayhem, murder, and blood. While he may not, generally speaking, reject drama as a literary form, he is strongly suggesting that although Lope may be the acknowledged master of the honor theme in plays (and at that, plays of a certain kind), in prose Cervantes could do as well artistically as Lope. Cervantes offers a truly Christian, humane view and solution to the question of soiled honor.

Chapter Five

Apologia pro patria sua
Cervantes's "La señora Cornelia"

The writing of "La señora Cornelia" was an attempt to salvage and protect an ideal picture of Spain that Cervantes held, one that the Spanish reading public also wished to preserve. I study in this tale the idea of Italy as cultural myth and ideal structure, with Spain cast as a negative image; and the final picture that emerges from the work is that of an *apologia pro patria sua* (Cervantes's), an image as ideal as its contrary image was false.

Because of the choice of the locale for the tale, this *novela* has been labeled as within the Italianate tradition.[1] The personal experiences of Cervantes, who had been in Italy as a chamberlain to the young Cardinal Acquaviva and who subsequently served in the militia there, are considered to be a source for this *novela*. Allusions to Italy and Italian life also appear in other *novelas* ("El licenciado Vidriera," "La fuerza de la sangre," and "La gitanilla") and may also depend to a certain degree on these biographical influences.

Jean Canavaggio highlights the influence in Cervantes of a literary tradition rather than a lived one: "Ce n'est pas l'amateur de 'choses vues,' mais le fin lecteur de Boccace et des *novellieri*" (74–75). Furthermore, he states:

> Le *Décaméron* de Boccace, et son extraordinaire variété de personnages et de situations: si l'auteur des *Nouvelles exemplaires* n'en a pas repris telle quelle la manière, il en a cependant retenu la leçon; sans sacrifier sa propre originalité, il en transposera si heureusement la formule que ses contemporains le surnommeront "le Boccace Espagnol." (79–80)

I accept those perceptive remarks in part because they localize Cervantes within a literary tradition to which I believe he belongs.[2]

121

Chapter Five

Juana Granados, however, sees some differences between the asserted Boccaccean sources and "La señora Cornelia": "però la burla e il ruolo della cameriera non riescono ad assumere quel tono scherzoso che è proprio della novella italiana" (66). In reviewing the characters of, and influences on, Cervantes's Italianate *novelas*, she sees them as "fra il boccaccesco e la lezione morale a lieto fine" (48). Earlier, Granados pointed to the influence of Italian writers on Cervantes (see 15–16).

There are several other possible sources. Still another tradition that must be highlighted but has not been developed is the tradition of the "vida estudiantil." Since the two Spanish characters are studying in Bologna, some of their episodes are easily recognized within the student-life tradition.[3] Yet another source of the *novela* is history itself: the characters of Cornelia Bentivoglio and Alfonso d'Este as well as the names of the two Basque gentlemen can be identified with real, historical figures.[4] As has been discussed earlier, Cervantes's work was intergeneric, and he has liberally availed himself of many other traditions. Boccaccio was the great model for the later Renaissance writers (as well as other *novellieri* whose work Cervantes knew well [Bandello, Masuccio, et al.]; see above, chapter 1). Canavaggio's observations convince me that one of Cervantes's approaches to this *novela* (and others) was literary (even though the description that the captain gives of Italy in "El licenciado Vidriera" could easily come from the actual experience that Cervantes had).[5]

It is difficult to identify specific incidents in Cervantes's biography with aspects of "La señora Cornelia," but given some historical events there is one aspect of his life that may be a key to some of the episodes. Croce, in his review of the Spanish presence in Italy, points to one feature that may account for Cervantes's presence in the group around Cardinal Acquaviva: "Per la stessa ragione [Spaniards] erano considerati 'maestri della cortegiania,' e ricercati nelle corti e soprattutto in quelle dei prelati di Roma: talché 'spagnuolo' e 'cortigiano' diventarono quasi sinonimi" (188). It was perhaps in this role that the Cardinal accepted Cervantes as a part of his retinue.

The results of Cardinal Acquaviva's choice of Cervantes as a page were far more felicitous than one might think. Cervantes's presence in such court and religious circles can reasonably be

Apologia pro patria sua

seen as of great importance for his literary formation. It was under the tutelage of Cardinal Acquaviva that Cervantes probably became familiar with many Italian authors whose works influenced his own writing.

While the presence of Italy in Cervantes's work is certainly justified by the time he spent there, the role of that country in "La señora Cornelia" and other *novelas* forces us to re-examine any strict link between his experience and the use he makes of Italy. With Cardinal Acquaviva, Cervantes visited Palermo, Venice, Rome, and Ferrara; he refers to Florence, Lucca, and Bologna. While in military service he visited several parts of Italy from Genoa to Venice, Rome, Naples, and Sicily. While there is no question of his presence or his powers of observation, the actual mention of Italy in the work is somewhat arbitrary. Rodríguez Luis notes that in "La señora Cornelia" it took three days to go to Ferrara and return, yet there are no descriptions of the trip or the areas the characters passed through (1: 92).

Tomás Rodaja, the Glass Licentiate, believes that travel makes men wise; travel to Italy was basic for the cultured person of the time. Casalduero notes, "Se va a Italia a sentir en toda su plenitud vital, en todas las dimensiones del espíritu, la cultura" (114). Yet, Casalduero also points out some inconsistencies in Cervantes's treatment of Italian space and locale: "Enumeraciones, nombres, atributos impuestos, pero no gastados; al contrario, llenos de expresión y cargados de fuerza ornamental" (116). For instance, with respect to Genoa, Casalduero states, "No hay creación de ambiente, no podía haberlo: esperarlo indica una total desorientación; lo que hay es una enumeración de ciudades con caracterización general" (115). The narrator talks about wines and women. He devotes three lines to Lucca; more or less the same to Florence. In Genoa he admires the blond women, the handsome men, and the beauty of the city. Rome is the great baroque city. What Florence was for the Renaissance, Rome would become as the great urban center of the Counter-Reformation (115–16). Amezúa notes with respect to the city of Bologna that the descriptions "no pueden ser más pobres e inexpresivos" (2: 363). Alfredo Giannini, according to Amezúa, notes, "aparte ciertos rasgos realmente italianos, como hacer al cura *piovano* amante de las artes, el

Chapter Five

colorido y la fisonomía del contenido de la novela cervantina son esencialmente español y nacionales" (2: 363). Canavaggio also associates the descriptions with other-than-real links: "Evocations habilement agencées, mais dont la charge symbolique transparaît à tout moment et qui, plutôt qu'elles ne plantent une succession de décors, proposent au lecteur une série d'emblèmes" (75).[6]

From the foregoing one can summarize that the Italy presented in "La señora Cornelia" (and other *novelas*) is not always a faithful description of the country, and the story could also take its departure from literary sources (Italian and Greek novelistic ones and the contemporary *comedia*).[7] Some of these reminiscences must surely coincide with Cervantes's own time spent in Italy and the experiences he had there, but ultimately the final presence in the tale is a complex one that is conditioned by different forms of human and intellectual experience. However, to be precise, the final meaning of Italy in "La señora Cornelia" corresponds, in my opinion, to a specific historical problem.

The choice of Italy as a locale for this *novela* was not an accident and corresponded to a specific awareness by both author and reading public. For many, Rome was the Holy See, which was not solely limited to religious and theological symbols but included greatness in art. Spaniards flocked to Italy, attracted by the ideal of humanism. Casalduero acknowledges the importance of the association of Rome and the Pope. He also points out that during "el viaje a Italia" (as he refers to Cervantes's stay in Italy), Rome was a great baroque center, the seat of ancient as well as Counter-Reformation Rome (113–15). Canavaggio believes that the ideal space of humanism and literature flourished in Italy, and Cervantes taught himself literature in Rome while in the retinue of Cardinal Acquaviva. In Naples, Pedro Laínez introduced him to several literary *cénacles* where he became aware of the work of Petrarch, Boiardo, Ariosto, and Boccaccio (Canavaggio 79). As Croce states it,

> Ma diversissimo poi nei rispetti della cultura, perché gl'italiani erano adusati a vedere gli spagnuoli presentarsi quali ammiratori e discepoli, e discepoli perfino umili, come già re Alfonso e i tanti signori e prelati e umanisti di quella gente, e mettersi a imparare dagli italiani i buoni studî e il buon

latino, e procurare di spogliare l'ispidezza barbarica, e talora da guerrieri tramutarsi in dotti e in poeti. (110)[8]

The status of Italian letters was so exalted from the time of Dante to the middle of the seventeenth century that people came from all over Europe to partake of the glory that was Renaissance and baroque Italy. Spain could not, as Croce notes, provide models for the Italians to emulate but rather Spain had to turn to Italy to borrow from that glorious tradition. No better examples could be found than Garcilaso and Cervantes himself. The Spanish humanists who wrote in Latin were regarded as inferior to the Italian humanists (Croce 174–75), and their work in this mode was to be looked upon as undergoing improvement in Italy. Not only was Italy and the ideal of humanism, letters, and learning sought after, but the great Aldine presses were publishing the works of Spanish writers like Alfonso de Valdés and the *Amadís* (Croce 164).

At the time that Cervantes underwent this experience in Italy, there was an image or ideal picture of Italy to be reckoned with. Cervantes, like so many of his compatriots, no doubt fell sway to this ideal, which permeated all of Europe. As Canavaggio sees it, Cervantes's Italy was "le fruit d'une expérience directe; elle est aussi, grâce au pouvoir des mots, un monde imaginaire où évoluent des êtres de fiction" (78); or even the image and attraction of Italy for Cervantes and others was a "Nostalgie d'une civilisation raffinée, donc, mais aussi d'une *dolce vita italiana* qui, à l'étranger capable de les apprécier, offre la gamme infinie de ses séductions" (76).

At the core of the *novela* is the wish of the Spanish characters to succumb to this image of Italy: "quisieron ver todas las más famosas ciudades de Italia; y habiéndolas visto todas pararon en Bolonia . . ." (2: 241). The choice of Bologna was a natural one, since Cardinal Gil de Albornoz had establishcd the Colegio Español there, which, not coincidentally for the *novela*, was excluded from Philip II's general pragmatic against studying abroad. That this Italian/Spanish equation in the *novela* was loaded in favor of the Italian side can be gleaned from Lorenzo's self-defensive statement: "—Yo, señor español, soy Lorenzo Bentibolli, si no de los más ricos, de los más principales desta ciudad" (2: 257). Further proof can be found when the *ama* is

Chapter Five

relating her life and, wishing to point to the nadir to which she has fallen, says, "—pues con ser quien soy [los Cribelos (Crivelli) de Milán], he venido a ser masara de españoles . . ." (2: 263).

Therefore Cervantes takes this image and "concept" of Italy and builds one side of an equation as an ideal power, looked up to, admired, and idealized. Cervantes's handling of the Spanish side of the equation is more complex and in my opinion is the answer to the riddle of the use of Italy in the *novela* in such positive terms.

Basically, the Italians looked down on the Spaniards. Buttressed by a privileged position in the world of spirituality and religion (the Holy See) and strengthened by the awesome influence of Italian letters in the world, the Italians regarded the Spaniards as people who came to Italy to learn. Moreover, the Spaniards (like the French) affected a "disprezzo per le 'lettere'" (Croce 116) that must have been very shocking to Italians, much of whose culture was tied to the word. A statement by Don Juan in the *novela* tips off the reader that in this *novela* the Spaniards are working at a disadvantage, i.e., they have a negative reputation, and it was best in some situations to disavow being Spanish ("dijo . . . en lengua italiana, por no ser conocido por español" [2: 245]).

The negative images of Spain permeated everyday life. As Croce points out, the expression "danari di Spagna" referred to empty wealth, money that never came. In literature, Spanish characters appear as boasters ("vantatori e millantatori" [Croce 187]). A "spagnolata" referred to "pompositá" and "fanfaronata" (Croce 187). This Spanish negative characteristic is associated with certain external modes and gestures. In the theater there is a Spanish character named Don Diego di Mendoza, known as the "Spagnuolo innamorato." An image of Spaniards is also to be found in the works of Pietro Aretino.[9]

Spaniards were also looked down upon for their insistence on externals, especially in their dress, which was viewed as "pompe e ricercatezza delle vesti e altri mali costumi" (Croce 121; see also 181). Croce notes: "Il vero è solamente questo: che gli spagnuoli, svolgendo il cerimoniale e promovendo l'amore per le dimostrazioni esteriori, dettero esempio e furono incentivo di stile cerimonioso e ingegnoso, gonfio e vuoto" (204–05). The text of "La señora Cornelia" reveals an awareness of the Spanish penchant for ceremony: "No acabó de decir esto el duque cuando

Apologia pro patria sua

don Juan, con extraña ligereza, saltó del caballo y acudió a besar los pies del duque" (2: 264). Shortly afterward, the narrator relates: "El señor Lorenzo [here, the Italian part of the equation], que desde algo lejos miraba estas ceremonias" (2: 264). The Spanish tendency toward such courtesy and gestures was ridiculed by Italians. Equally Don Lorenzo says, revealing Cervantes's awareness of the Spanish inclination to ceremony, "—Suplico a vuecencia—que ésta es la merced de Italia" (2: 256). Along with the stress on ceremony went the Spanish use of titles, many of which became assimilated into Italian life, e.g., the use of *Señor, Don,* and other titles. Croce notes, "quantunque taluno movesse protesta affermando che in Ispagna ce n'era l'uso e in Italia l'abuso" (196). Expressions of obvious Spanish origin also came into the language: "bacio le mani" (Croce 196). Amezúa wisely points out that Cervantes in this *novela* does not attach to the Spanish characters a widely perceived Spanish trait: "la famosa y tan censurada arrogancia española" (2: 365). Gianbattista Marino, whose language was not beyond *hinchazón,* referred to Spanish dances generally as "giochi empi e profani" (cited by Croce 199).[10] Giovanni Giraldi Cinzio urged that writers avoid Spanish uses of language

> "schivare que' mostruosi modi di dire, che sono oggidí si pregiati da molti che non pure nelle commedie e nelle tragedie, ma ne' domestici parlari e nelle stesse famigliari lettere gli hanno in guisa sparsi, che in ogni foglio se ne trovano due o tre." (Cited by Croce 205)

The Spanish occupation of the Italian peninsula must be viewed in stages. There was an early stage where the Spanish imperial idea brought to other countries its best and most noble representatives. However, in Cervantes's time, the Italian peninsula saw the arrival of soldiery of all kinds, and not always the best people (Croce 240). Italy has always held an attraction for Spanish and Catalan adventurers (Croce 15). Croce notes, "nel loro paese non avevano né casa né possessione e si cibavano di pane e ravanelli e bevevano acqua, e in Italia erano venuti con le scarpe di corda" (186). He also cites the cases of Don García Enríquez de Guzmán, who at 19 years of age left Seville "a buscar sus aventuras" (239), and Pedro de Navarro, "recatosi in Italia a cercar fortuna come staffiere del cardinale

Chapter Five

Giovanni d'Aragona" (277). Italy, quite apart from its humanistic attractions, could also be looked upon as a "lieu de l'aventure," as Canavaggio calls it (75), which was as attractive to Cervantes as to anyone else, including the Basque subjects of the *novela*. Luis Astrana Marín quotes Vasco Díaz de Fregenal, who states,

> Los seis aventureros de España, y como el uno va a las Indias, y el otro a Italia, y el otro a Flandes, y el otro está preso, y el otro anda entre pleitos, y el otro entra en religión. E como en España no hay más gente destas seis personas sobredichas. (*Vida ejemplar* 219)

The placement of the work in Italy with its particular adventurous overtones was hardly an accident on Cervantes's part, and the characters' link with adventure was not a *novedad* for the seventeenth-century reader. Croce views this situation in the following way:

> Tale era l'atteggiamento degli spagnuoli, consapevoli della loro potenza, inebriati della loro buona fortuna, orgogliosi delle loro forze e virtù di fronte agli italiani, misuranti ormai il proprio popolo con l'altro e sentendo la propria superiorità e creando per esso perfino una preistoria o leggenda. (110)

This was essentially the image that both Spaniards and Italians alike had of the Spanish imperial dream, a dream of power and strength. But with time the reality of this image began to crack and decay. After the great moment of adventure, Croce observes, "La Spagna, invece d'inviare in Italia, come ai primi tempi, uomini di guerra arditi e avventurosi, inviava magistrati esperti nello spremere i popoli e nel tenerli a freno col rigore o con gli accorgimenti e le blandizie e la 'grascia'" (265). At this later stage of the Spanish presence, which coincides with Cervantes's stay in Italy: "Sotto il dominio spagnuolo crebbero nelle città italiane le plebi oziosi e cenciose coi luridi vizî della miseria, e la lingua spagnuola fornì allora al dialetto napoletano le tre parole... *lazzaro, guappo e camorrista*" (Croce 266). This moment also is characterized by a change from lively Renaissance literary models to the models of treatises of preachers and spiritual books. The adventurous spirit of the much read *libros de caballerías* is replaced by a different view, conditioned no doubt by a counterreformistic atmosphere.[11]

In spite of a negative Italian attitude toward Catalans,[12] Croce views aspects of the Italo-Hispanic *convivencia* as "è da riconoscere che un vero odio nazionale contro la Spagna e gli spagnuoli non ci fu in Italia durante quel secolo e mezzo, e sta di fatto che la loro potenza cadde e disparve dell'Italia per cagioni non già nazionali ma internazionali" (262).

Returning for support of this idea to the *novela* itself, note once again that the *ama* views her lowest point as having to serve Spaniards, especially since she hails from the family of the Crivelli of Milan (2: 263), or even that Lorenzo Bentibolli says, as Rodríguez Luis observes, "Lorenzo, un italiano solicite la ayuda de los vizcaínos, lo primero en que repara el ama" (102).[13] But another clue to the particular polemical nature of the *novela* is the rejection by the Basque students of the invitation to take Italian wives, a solution as antithetical as it is aesthetically unjustified (see 2: 276–77). In terms of the binomial rivalry, Cervantes has the Spanish half of the equation prevail. The students reject the invitation politely ("Ellos dijeron que los caballeros de la nación vizcaína por la mayor parte se casaban en su patria" [2: 276–77]). In the final phrase rejecting the Italian marriages, Cervantes, tongue-in-cheek, has the narrator add "no aceptaban tan *ilustre* [emphasis mine] ofrecimiento" (2: 277). *Ilustre* can only be read ironically, and the Spanish pride is safely retained.

Cervantes, as a Spaniard in Italy, no doubt found himself identified with numerous stereotypes, many of which were negative. When Cervantes has the captain sing the praises of Italian life, it is, of course, a form of idealism. How many readers in fact like Cervantes had been in Italy and had succumbed to the lure of that country? The *novela*, with its latent polemic of Spanish life being viewed through Italian negativism, has to defend Spain, and providing that defense is the function of the Basque noblemen.[14]

Italian contacts with Spanish life hark back to the Middle Ages. There is a lively interchange over the centuries of Italians responding to Spanish culture. Ariosto claims to have translated Spanish and French novels in his youth (Croce 169).

Chapter Five

The popularity of *Amadís, Celestina,* and other major works would argue for at least some recognition of humanistic worth (even if the Italians felt themselves to be superior to the Spanish and their culture). At a relatively early moment Catalans emigrated to Italy and maintained a lively presence, even though Croce points to an Italian odium for Catalans (Croce 28). While the Italians could boast of the importance of Aldine presses, the Valencians could also boast of the lively book trade, which included translations and the works of the great Italian writers.

During the era of Alphonse of Aragon the immigration of Spaniards takes on a particular intensity and meaning. Another wave of immigration accompanied Cardinal Borja and his retinue. Among many, Alfonso de Cartagena, Bishop of Burgos, came to Italy in search of the great culture it possessed, and Pietro Martire and Andrea Navagero went to Spain.[15] The overwhelming emigration was of Spaniards to Italy for numerous reasons, politics being the most obvious and the most important. In fact, the Spanish presence became so widespread that its influence overwhelmed cities like Genoa, Naples, Rome, and Messina.[16] Nicolas Audebert notes that about 1577 the number of Spaniards in Naples was equal to the number of Italians (Croce 235). At the time when Garcilaso went to Italy, numerous Spanish families had become almost permanent fixtures in Italian life: Alarcóns, Leyvas, Toledos, Borgias, Quiñones, Enríquez.[17] When Juan del Encina's play *Plácida y Victoriano* was mounted at the home of Cardinal Arborense, two-thirds of those present were Spaniards (Croce 163). Aretino assimilated Spanish characters into his plays (Croce 156 ff.). The response to the Spanish presence must have been overwhelming, for Croce observes,

> Quanto di spagnuolo era già in Italia, e particolarmente in Napoli e in Roma, si ravvivò e si dilatò in quei primi anni del secolo; e la Spagna parve allora invadere l'Italia non solo con le sue armi, ma con tutto il suo spirito nazionale, sforzando la tradizione, il costume e la cultura stessa italiana. (112)

In terms of the Spaniards' own self-picture, one could recall the phrase of the great Captain Gonzalo de Córdoba: "España las armas e Italia la pluma" (Croce 215 ff.).

Apologia pro patria sua

Cervantes structures a Spanish pride *sui generis* through his youthful, adventurous Basque heroes. These characters, according to Amezúa, were to be seen as examples of "perfección física y moral" (2: 356). Cervantes had presumably the wish to create the "idealización del tipo del caballero español a que Cervantes aspira en esta novela" (Amezúa 2: 365). But this creation was not without a particular use and purpose. Amezúa avers:

> Nuestros buenos mancebos vizcaínos refrenarán empero este orgullo, en aquella idealización del tipo del caballero español a que Cervantes aspira en esta novela, uno de aquellos momentos de su concepción novelística en que él se aparta de la realidad para buscar la ejemplaridad propuesta, pues la ejemplaridad no sólo se consigue en los venturosos desenlaces, donde la virtud es premiada y castigado el vicio, sino mostrando también al lector cómo los personajes concebidos deben ser en su vida y costumbres, para que así sirvan de modelo y dechado a todos. (2: 365–66)[18]

What is striking about the Spanish representation in the *novela* is its link with nobility. Together with the Italian side, a world of superior values is identified. Don Juan says, "—Si hasta aquí, hermosa señora, yo y don Antonio, mi camarada, os teníamos compasión y lástima por ser mujer, ahora, que sabemos vuestra *calidad* [emphasis mine], la lástima y compasión pasa a ser obligación precisa de serviros" (2: 254).

Lorenzo also acknowledges the nobility of the pair, a nobility that is indivisible from being Spanish. He says, "—que me acompañásedes en este camino, confiado en que lo haréis por ser español y caballero. . . . Vos, señor, me habéis de hacer merced de venir conmigo, que llevando un español a mi lado, y tal como vos me parecéis . . ." (2: 258).

The characters, including the Italian ones, all seem to be in agreement concerning the ideal of Spanish nobility and courtesy, for Cornelia is quoted as saying, " '—Podría ser que el que traigo lo fuese, si presto no se me da remedio; por la cortesía que siempre suele reinar en los de vuestra nación, os suplico, señor español, que me saquéis destas calles' " (2: 247).[19] An interesting detail should get our attention, because it reveals the substratum of Don Antonio's pride as a nobleman. When, as he recounts, he is asked by Cornelia, " '—¿Por ventura, señor,

Chapter Five

sois extranjero o de la ciudad?' " he answers, " '—Extranjero soy y español . . .' " (2: 247). Focusing on Don Juan, El Saffar notes, "Don Juan throws himself into life and the story because of his noble spirit. It is his faith in his honor and in justice that leads him into action which might otherwise look dangerous" (*Novel to Romance* 122). There are further examples in the text that point to an effort on Cervantes's part to highlight the Spaniards in a very positive light. Consider the words of Cornelia:

> —y aunque me veo sin hijo y sin esposo y con temor de peores sucesos, doy gracias al cielo, que me ha traído a vuestro poder, de quien me prometo todo aquello que de la cortesía española puedo prometerme, y más de la vuestra, que la sabéis realzar por ser tan nobles como parecéis. (2: 253)

Amezúa comments:

> Otro de los valores españoles de aquel tiempo que resalta en *La señora Cornelia* es la generosidad y bizarría con que un caballero se lanza a la defensa de una causa noble atropellada, y arriesga su misma persona, sin considerar el peligro en que se pone. (2: 366)

Contrary to what Italians may have fixed in their minds about Spanish manners, Cervantes presents a completely different picture: "Oyendo y viendo lo cual don Juan, llevado de su valeroso corazón, en dos brincos se puso al lado, y metiendo mano a la espada y a un broquel que llevaba, dijo al que defendía, en lengua italiana, por no ser conocido por español" (2: 244–45). Rather than see Don Juan as trying to avoid an identification with Spain by speaking Italian, paradoxically, here his ability serves to intensify his achievement. He is shown as a Spanish nobleman, who, having mastered Italian, can therefore deal with Italians on a completely equal linguistic level.

While Italian mores may have taken the Spanish nobleman and caricatured him, especially in the area of love, Cervantes has Cornelia strongly point to the good manners of the Spanish:

> y en tanto que comían dio cuenta Cornelia de todo lo que le había sucedido hasta venir a aquella casa por consejo de la ama de los dos caballeros españoles, que la habían servido, amparado y guardado con el más honesto y puntual decoro que pudiera imaginarse. (2: 274)

Apologia pro patria sua

There is still another aspect of the characterization of the young Spanish noblemen, a characteristic that we might find only with difficulty in comparable Italian *novelle*, and that is a sense of spirituality and religiosity: "dijo don Antonio a don Juan que él se quería quedar a rezar ciertas devociones . . ." (2: 243).[20]

Thus does Cervantes juxtapose an ideal vision of Spain and Spaniards by creating a scenario of a Spaniard defending the patrimony before another culture. Cervantes's gesture is particularly meaningful at a time when Spain was beset by numerous problems, political and economic ones among others, and at a time when Spain's power was waning. (I am assuming that the tale was written after his Italian experience and his imprisonment in Algiers.) The story is aimed at other Spaniards who, like Cervantes, can see a picture of a Spain that *was* rather than a Spain that *is*.

Given the Italian/Spanish equation, special attention must be given to the use Cervantes makes of Italian in "La señora Cornelia" (and also in "El licenciado Vidriera"). He names the central characters Lorenzo and Cornelia Bentibolli, an obvious redoing of the Italian Bentivoglio. Reference is made to the Crivellis of Milan (Cribelos in the text).[21] What is striking is that neither of these are in correct Italian. Even in "El licenciado Vidriera" we see "dibujóle dulce y puntualmente el *aconcha, patrón; pasa acá, manigoldo; venga la macarela, li polastri e li macaroni*" (2: 45; emphasis in original).

On the one hand one could acknowledge Croce who, focusing on the Spanish presence in Naples, noted the confluence in language of "spagnolerie" and "napolitanerie" (189). He also states, "E, in effetti, verso la metà del secolo Napoli sembrava già, quanto a lingua, un paese mezzo spagnuolo" (158). Spanish words came into Italian, e.g., *mozzo, mucciaccio* (Croce 156, 160).[22]

One must acknowledge that in the service of Cardinal Acquaviva, Cervantes was exposed to Italian life in all its forms. Is it reasonable to believe that Cervantes, who had read the Italian authors, both poets and writers of prose, would not know that the character's name is Bentivoglio and not the Italian *sounding* (emphasis mine) Bentibolli? Cervantes had read all of the great Italian Renaissance writers, and the Italian presence in

133

Chapter Five

his writing would rule out something as simple as the mispronunciation of a name like Bentivoglio. But *Las novelas ejemplares* was written for the Spanish public that may, like Cervantes himself, have been in Italy either in military service or, like the millions across Europe at the time, have made the perfunctory cultural trip either to the Holy See at Rome or to contemplate the artistic greatness of such Italian cities as Florence or Venice. Cervantes used Italian much as G.I.'s used German, Italian, Japanese, Korean, or Vietnamese words. His use of Italian must have been a gentle stroking of the memory of those who had been in Italy, and at the same time, perhaps like Cervantes they, too, had been looked at askance by Italians who regarded them as vacuous boors, exemplary on the outside but empty on the inside: "gonfio e vuoto." Out of a deep sense of pride, Cervantes creates a tale in which the "good guys" are ideal configurations of Spaniards and their comportment the best that could be produced by their culture. Glimpsing the decline of that same one-time great culture, Spain, Cervantes performs an act of patriotism and painful recollection. It is the recreation of the "grandeza española" in an era that is hardly grand any more.

Notes

Introduction

1. See Américo Castro's seminal remarks on the subject in his *El pensamiento de Cervantes*, 230-39, as well as Blanco Aguinaga's influential "Cervantes y la picaresca."
2. See my article "Cervantes y Mateo Alemán: de nuevo."
3. See my "Cervantes and the Picaresque: Redivivo."
4. There are several important studies that treat the subject of reader, public, and generally reader response: Edward C. Riley's fundamental *Cervantes's Theory of the Novel;* Robert Alter's *Partial Magic: The Novel as a Self-Conscious Genre*, especially his chapter on Don Quijote, "Mirror of Knighthood, World of Mirrors"; Ruth El Saffar's *Distance and Control;* see especially Dominick Finello's excellent *Pastoral Themes and Forms in Cervantes's Fiction*, especially under the themes *nobility* and *eclogue*.

Chapter One
"La gitanilla":
At the Crossroads
of History and Creativity

1. Leblon, *Les Gitans de la littérature espagnole* 93-94 (hereafter referred to as *Lit.* to distinguish it from *Les Gitans d'Espagne*, also by Leblon, which will be referred to as *Gitans*). See also Grande, *Memoria del flamenco* 99. These dates are taken from the *Novísima recopilación*, lib. 12, leyes 1, 2, and 3; cited by Sánchez Ortega 25 ff. For the role of Charles V in matters relating to Gypsies, see Covarrubias: "y fuera de ser ladrones manifiestos, que roban en el campo y en poblado, de algunos dellos se puede presumir que son espías, y por sospecha de ser tales los mandó desterrar de toda Alemaña el emperador Carlos V, año de mil quinientos y quarenta y nueve, en la dieta que tuvo en Augusta, cap. 26" (642b).

2. In "La gitanilla," in two instances, reference is made to Philip II: "Mira, niña, que andamos en oficio muy peligroso y lleno de tropiezos y de ocasiones forzosas, y no hay defensas que más presto nos amparen y socorran como las armas invencibles del gran Filipo" (1: 88); "de cuando la reina nuestra señora Margarita salió a misa de parida en Valladolid" (1: 67). It is hard for me to believe that Cervantes is idly mentioning the name of Philip II, this same Philip II that is responsible for the continued repressions of Gypsies. As a consequence of the above, we have a good example of what happens to Gypsies who run afoul of the law: "Tres veces por tres delitos diferentes me he visto casi puesta en el asno para ser azotada" (1: 88). See also *Novísima recopilación*, lib. 12, leyes 1, 2, and 3; cited by Sánchez Ortega 25 ff.

3. Since the phrase was modeled on the earlier "cristianos nuevos," with the attendant social stigma, it is hard to believe that in the fifteenth

135

or sixteenth centuries this nomenclature did not have the same pejorative connotations that Sánchez Ortega speaks of in the eighteenth century; see 76.

4. "y para dar cumplimiento a referido y se castigue semejante género de gente foragidos, y otros, que se dicen, y llaman Gitanos, que no lo son, ni por origen, ni naturaleza, hablando lengua jerigonza, haciendo trueques, y cambios de cabalgaduras y cometen delitos de los expresados, que estos con solo el nombre Gitanos, por Reales Pragmáticas, están sentenciados a Galeras" (Sánchez Ortega 126). Cervantes's work reflects this preoccupation in the person of Andrés. Preciosa says to him: "y la [casa de sus padres] habéis de trocar con nuestros ranchos, y tomando el traje de gitano, habéis de cursar dos años en nuestras escuelas" (1: 86). Andrés says, "Cuando el cielo me dispuso para quererte . . . cuéntame por gitano desde luego" (1: 86). See 1: 66 for the ceremonies that accompany Andrés's induction into the Gypsy band through which he becomes a novice Gypsy.

5. That this feature of Gypsy life was not overlooked by Cervantes, cf. the following: "—Par Dios, señor Andrés—dijo uno de los gitanos—, que aunque la mula tuviera más señales que las que han de preceder al día tremendo, aquí la transformáramos de manera que no lo conociera la madre que la parió, ni el dueño que la ha criado" (1: 99) and "y si de aquí a dos horas la [mula] conociere, que me lardeen como a un negro fugitivo" (1: 100). See also Covarrubias: ". . . Gitanería, qualquiera agudeza o presteza hecha en esta ocasión, porque los gitanos son grandes trueca burras, y en su poder parecen las bestias una cebras, y en llevándolas el que las compra, son más lerdas que tortugas" (643a).

6. "Si bien no fue específicamente perseguida por la Inquisición, como es el caso de las restantes minorías, fue el objeto principal de la atención de la Santa Hermandad" (Sánchez Ortega 102); "La inquisición no se preocupó de ellos con la intensidad con que se preocupó y persiguió a moriscos y judaizantes. Al parecer, los tenía en muy inferior concepto, y sólo en casos muy individuales, particulares y escandalosos sentó la mano" (Clébert 305).

7. See Clébert 300. Starkie notes a difference regarding the creation of the term *castellanos nuevos* "to distinguish them from their nomadic brothers, the 'Gitanos bravíos' or 'fierce Gypsies'" (338).

8. "Devenues paysans, sédentaires, disséminés dans des agglomérations importantes, dans l'impossibilité de se déplacer et donc de se rencontrer, les Gitans devaient se fondre rapidement dans la masse des travailleurs comme quelques descendants de Juifs et Morisques avaient pu le faire avant eux" (Leblon, *Gitans* 54–56).

9. See Casalduero 42; Caro Baroja, Epilogue/Prologue 294. Cf. Cervantes: "Salió la tal Preciosa la más única bailadora que se hallaba en todo el gitanismo, y la más hermosa y discreta que pudiera hallarse, no entre los gitanos, sino entre cuantas hermosas y discretas pudiera pregonar la fama" (1: 61); "Salió Preciosa rica de villancicos, de coplas, seguidillas

Notes to Pages 22–24

y zarabandas, y de otros versos, especialmente de romances, que los cantaba con especial donaire" (1: 62); "Tomó las sonajas Preciosa, y dieron sus vueltas, hicieron y deshicieron todos sus lazos, con tanto donaire y desenvoltura, que tras los pies se llevaban los ojos de cuantos las miraban . . ." (1: 95); on the enchanting effects of music and dance, see "Esta [Juana Carducha], habiendo visto bailar a las gitanas y gitanos, la tomó el diablo, y se enamoró de Andrés tan fuertemente . . ." (1: 122).

10. Concerning magic and Gypsies, see Covarrubias: "Harto está dicho desta ruin gente; el que quisiere ver más por estenso lo que es su origen y su trato, vea al padre Martín del Río en sus Disquisiciones Mágicas, lib. 4, cap. 3, q. 6" (643a); as well as "las mugeres son grandes ladronas y embustidoras, que dizen la buenaventura por las rayas de las manos, y en tanto que ésta tiene embevidas a las necias, con si se han de casar o parir o topar con buen marido, las demás dan buelta a la casa y se llevan lo que pueden" (643a). The Gypsies' penchant for magic and magic rituals is well known. In "La gitanilla," Cervantes gives us three examples: "Y haciéndole [Andrés] media docena de cruces sobre el corazón, se apartó dél, y entonces Andrés respiró un poco y dió a entender que las palabras de Preciosa le habían aprovechado" (1: 97); "Cuando la gitana vieja oyó el ensalmo y el embuste, quedó pasmada, y más lo quedó Andrés, que vio que todo era invención de su agudo ingenio" (1: 98); "Tomó algunos pelos de los perros, friólos en aceite, y, lavando primero con vino dos mordeduras que tenía en la pierna izquierda, le puso los pelos con el aceite en ellas, y encima un poco de romero verde mascado" (1: 109).

11. See the following: "Preciosa, dime la buenaventura" (1: 82). See also Francisco Márquez Villanueva's comment: "La buenaventura se ha vuelto una denuncia integral, burla deshumanizadora que arranca, una tras otra, las hojas de parra y sucesivamente expone a vista de todos las vergüenzas corporales del teniente y de su esposa. Tras ello, un verdadero ensañamiento sacará también a relucir las faltas de conducta privada y hasta las lacras de la misma sangre" ("La buenaventura de Preciosa" 750).

12. See 337. Preciosa gives us a good indication of this proverb when she says: "Los ingenios de las gitanas van por otro norte que los de las demás gentes: siempre se adelantan a sus años; no hay gitano necio, ni gitana lerda; que como el sustentar su vida consiste en ser agudos, astutos y embusteros, despabilan el ingenio a cada paso, y no dejan que críe moho en ninguna manera. . . . No hay muchacha de doce que no sepa lo que de veinte y cinco, porque tienen por maestros y preceptores al diablo y al uso, que les enseña en una hora lo que habían de aprender en un año" (1: 76–77).

13. For at least two instances of the myth of freedom as associated with Gypsy life see Leblon, *Gitans* 48 and *Lit.* 193. See also Forcione for whom "freedom" and "nature" are ambivalent terms in Cervantes (178, 192n178).

Notes to Pages 25–31

14. Leblon is conservative with respect to Cervantes's humanitarian impulses toward Gypsies: "La béatification des Gitans est un entreprise parfaitement impossible au XVII siècle, et Cervantes a suffisamment montré que telle n'était pas son intention. Faire de ces 'barbares' le dernier avatar du *Beatus ille,* c'était saboter et faire sombrer irrémédiablement le thème horatien du retour à la nature" (*Lit.* 199). I, however, go further than he does.

15. Rosales 6b, c. For another view of the artistic point of view of "La gitanilla," see Selig 273–74. I can assume that the three facets that Rosales sees represented the artistic structure upon which Cervantes could build.

16. It is easy for a twentieth-century reader to look for "revolutionary" gestures on important social and human issues. However, the reality of Cervantes's seventeenth-century life is not so easy. See Laspéras, who comments on "Cervantes—revolucionario." While he says "l'auteur des *Novelas ejemplares* se livre à une activité de déconstruction des images que lui proposent la culture et la langue" (354); he also says that Cervantes is not "contestataire que l'on s'est plu parfois à dépeindre" (435).

17. See Casalduero 53.

18. See also Leblon, *Lit.* 184; Gypsies never took Communion. He sees in Gypsies and *moriscos* theft and lack of religion; they practiced common-law marriage, received no dispensations, no sacraments, kept no images, rosaries, papal bulls, celebrated no masses. Citing T. Cesareo, Leblon shows Cesareo's belief that the Gypsies were "profanateurs d'églises" and that they committed "les actes charnels de leurs concubinages dans ces asiles sacrés, puis qu'ils y dorment la nuit" (*Gitans* 53).

19. See Leblon, *Lit.* 122: "On a déjà vu, que, pour mendier, les Gitans prenaient soin de montrer qu'ils étaient chrétiens. Cette préoccupation demeure, car les Gitans resteront toujours suspects aux yeux de l'Eglise." He further states that in a report, the Gypsies "ne sont pas chrétiens, puis qu'ils n'observent aucune pratique religieuse, et en conclut qu'ils sont pires que les 'Morisques'" (*Lit.* 167).

20. Starkie offers a view of such marriages that contradicts Moncada: "He who marries a Gypsy girl marries everyone in the tribe, and the advantages and privileges which the *faraona,* or Gypsy princess, obtains are shared with the whole clan. In this way Romanichals have grafted their stock on many of the great noble families in the countries where they have halted" (339).

21. See Laspéras passim, for his ideas on Christian and Tridentine marriage as well as Bataillon's seminal "Cervantès et 'le mariage chrétien.'"

22. This is not to be confused with Castro's view of the picaresque genre as "negative idealism." Cervantes's manipulation here is intended to "reverse" the field of values, using the same terms that normally are applicable to conventionally admired groups.

23. See above Laspéras's comments on the unlikely role of Cervantes as a social revolutionary.

24. Leblon, *Lit.* 195. El Saffar astutely notes, "Preciosa, in *La gitanilla* sings and dances for a group of noble men and women who are too penurious to pay her anything. They are shown to be vain, selfish, and exploitive of Preciosa's talents" (*Novel to Romance* 21), as well as the fact that the Gypsy world offers a critical view of certain obvious defects in courtly life (90).

25. In assessing various extraliterary influences Forcione sees Cervantes's own conjectured marginality, a person of *converso* background, as a possible consideration (176); otherwise he is quite negative on Castro's point of literary-historical method (see 118n45, 171). I, on the other hand, would see Cervantes's *converso* origin, were it verifiable, as a major influence. This would then provide greater understanding for his sympathy regarding various marginal peoples, in this case, Gypsies; another case is that of Ricote the Moor.

26. Cervantes does this in "Rinconete y Cortadillo" with the thieves' guild, where there is no Cervantine social satire, but rather the treatment of a literary genre—the picaresque.

27. See Durán, who, quoting Casalduero, believes that a "naturalistic" agenda was the last thing on Cervantes's mind and that he did not have the purpose of portraying a social reality (60).

Chapter Two
Católicos secretos, Conversos, and the Myth of the Maritime Life in "La española inglesa"

1. While I do not embrace completely the particular economic interpretation that Johnson gives, I do accept wholeheartedly his historical approach.

2. The name of the Earl of Essex is more than a mere historical fact. The historical echoes of Cádiz resonate throughout Spanish history. Antonio Coello wrote a play based on the figure of the Earl of Essex, *El conde de Sex*. Coello was active as a dramatist around 1632 (admittedly, several years after the publication of the *Novelas ejemplares*). In that year Coello's play *El celoso extremeño* was presented by the theatrical company of Manuel Alvarez Vallejo, who later produced *El conde de Sex* (Coello, Schmiedel ed. 10). It is most probable that the public that welcomed Coello's play about the Earl of Essex also welcomed Cervantes's *novela* that involved the same person.

3. Montrose offers an interesting insight into this difficult situation. Focusing on an Armada portrait of Elizabeth I, he analyzes a detail in the painting. He says: "This demure iconography of Elizabeth's virgin-knot suggests a causal relationship between her sanctified chastity and the providential destruction of the Spanish Catholic invaders—an event represented in the background of the painting" (315). He further states: "The threat of invasion is here presented in the most intimate and violent of metaphors, as the attempted rape of the queen by a foreign prince" (315).

4. See also Holmes (209) and Plowden (17, 34), for other useful insights concerning Spain and Elizabethan England.

5. Holmes makes the following suggestion: "To adapt a phrase of Professor Elton there was no 'high road' to Catholic extinction, and the Elizabethans regarded Popery as immeasurably more dangerous than Puritanism. Indeed, the threat of Catholicism, with its international ramifications, its connection with the question of the succession, and its insidious danger to internal security, may be seen as the central and most important theme in the history of Elizabeth's reign" (7).

6. Ricaredo says: "Besé los pies al Sumo Pontífice, confesé mis pecados con el mejor penitenciero, absolviéndome dellos, y dióme los recaudos necesarios que diesen fe de mi confesión y penitencia y de la reducción que había hecho a nuestra universal madre la iglesia" (1: 279); as well as "Pedí confesión y todos los sacramentos como católico cristiano" (1: 280).

7. When Arnesto's mother is punished by the Queen for having administered poison to Isabel, the narrator explains her rationalization: "Mandó la reina prender a su camarera y encerrarle en un aposento estrecho de palacio, con intención de castigarla como su delito merecía, puesto que ella se disculpaba diciendo que en matar a Isabela hacía sacrificio al cielo, quitando de la tierra a una católica, y con ella la ocasión de las pendencias de su hijo" (1: 269).

8. In 1581, Persons published his treatise *De persecutione Anglicana.* This and other works described the persecution of Catholics in England. Later works by Allen, Richard Verstegan, John Gibbons, and others continued this process (Holmes 47).

9. It should not be forgotten that the new seminary priests who returned to England to proselytize and do missionary work were trained under the influence of the Counter-Reformation and were not ready to make any compromises (Morey 148).

10. See below for further observations concerning Elizabeth and James I. See also Campbell: "James drastically reduced the amount of recusancy fines leveled and seemed to favor a very lenient policy toward the Catholics. James's whole attitude and conduct, within his own court as well as in public affairs, showed that he could be a thoroughly reasonable man with a very practical outlook on religious differences. But Parliament interpreted this as either weakness or sympathy for Rome and refused to tolerate any move towards compromise with the papists" (39). Watkin notes that the persecution of Catholics during the time 1603–58 was sporadic: "James I, it is true, did not honour promises of toleration made when he sought Catholic support for his claim to the English succession" (62).

11. There is reasonable precedent for this symbolic interpretation. See Aylward's perceptive and original work.

12. See also: "There were churches that kept the forbidden equipment for celebrating Mass, where everything was ready 'to set up Mass again within twenty hours' warning,' where churchwardens concealed Catholic furnishings but certified them as destroyed. Bishop Bentham of Coventry had no doubt that many were 'hoping and looking for a new day as may thereby be conjectured.' The continuance in benefices of priests who were often prepared to say Mass privately before conducting the new service made things easier for the Catholic who was willing to attend church. So late as 1582 the charge was brought that 'Sir Miles Yare, parson of Sturson near Skole in Suffolk, sayeth Mass commonly in his parlour chamber in his own house and also . . . that in the said chamber are all things necessary pertaining thereto.' In the early years of the reign the bishops sometimes turned a blind eye to the superficial conformity of some of their clergy, and Bishop Downham of Chester allowed them great freedom" (Morey 44).

13. One should not forget that this same process of secrecy and secret adherence to faith could describe in an earlier time Spanish Christians of reformist tendencies.

14. See p. 46 for Casalduero's pertinent remarks. If this work were written for Spanish readers with Spaniards in make-believe roles, what particular good would it have done, historically, religiously, or aesthetically, since Protestantism as a polemic waned throughout the middle years of the sixteenth century, while the obsession with Jewish ancestry continued on well into the seventeenth century?

15. It is true that Ricaredo uses this as a ruse to not be unfaithful to Isabel, but the reference to Rome is not a jest and would not be made lightly.

16. Readers may be facing an interesting interpretation as far as names are concerned. The main female character is Isabela and the Queen's name translates to "Isabela." Since sympathy and benevolence is not one of the principal characteristics of Elizabeth Tudor, is it possible that Cervantes is invoking this quality, benevolence, as a reminiscence of Isabel la Católica?

17. I do not wish to become involved here in whether Cervantes was or was not a *converso*. I see him as a member of Spanish society subject to the whims, prejudices, pressures, etc., of society. He utilizes his gifts to view critically his own society and converts his ideas, feelings, passions into the written word. Nevertheless, see Angel M. García Gómez's interesting "Una historia sefardí como posible fuente de *La española inglesa* de Cervantes" as well as Manuel da Costa Fontes's lucid "Love as an Equalizer in *La española inglesa*."

18. "So, in spite of the long indecisive war which followed, the defeat of the Spanish Armada really was decisive. It decided that religious unity was not to be reimposed by force on the heirs of medieval Christendom, and if in doing so it only validated what was already by far the most probable outcome—why, perhaps that is all that any of the battles we

call decisive had ever done" (Mattingly 357). For students of Cervantes's life, a statement of Altamira's with respect to the insufficiency of supplies should have particular resonance: "Al amparo del desarreglo en la organización, los proveedores de la escuadra abusaron de manera gravísima, suministrando víveres en mal estado, que pronto quedaban inútiles" (3: 103–04).

19. See Greenblatt, 28, who focuses on a similar example of dress with reference to Elizabeth I and associates it with a theatrical metaphor. In Cervantes's example of this description of Isabel there is a similar example of a static, pictorial, iconographic motif.

20. Johnson, " 'La española inglesa' " 383; see also 396 for further statements to this effect. It must be said in Johnson's defense that he does link the economic principle with a religious one: "Finally, we are again in the presence of what we have called the 'catholic' economy, an advanced system of exchange based on credit, on mediation, on charity (that is, on love of one's fellow man) and on universality, and here at least involving the direct participation of the Roman Catholic Church" (406).

21. Johnson further states, "The change in ownership of the houses (the locus of prestige) across from Santa Paula (the locus of belonging) concretizes within text the triumphant emergence of a new class, the urban bourgeoisie, to replace the aristocracy as the protagonist of history" (" 'La española inglesa' " 415). This is another example of the "economic reality" of the work, and he goes on to posit several other economic hypotheses (see 415).

22. The reader might justifiably argue that the name is different, R*i*caredo as opposed to R*e*caredo. However, there are two instances where the name Ricaredo appears: Rikaredo and Richaredus. See Joseph M. Piel and Dieter Kremer, *Hispano-gotisches Namenbuch* 224, #16: "[Recaredus Westgotenkönige . . . Rikaredo 937 AC 109 . . . Richaredus 990 AC 224 . . .]." I am particularly grateful to S. G. Armistead for his generous assistance on this point.

23. See Bleiberg's *Diccionario de historia de España*. See also Thompson 113: "Recaredo se convirtió al catolicismo hacia febrero de 587 y fue bautizado *secretamente* [emphasis mine]."

24. See Menéndez Pidal, ed., *Primera crónica general* 1: 263b. This source also details Recaredo's valor: "Este rey Recaredo lidio muchas uezes con los romanos et con los gascones quel crebantauan la tierra et ge la robauan, et uencio los siempre" (1: 264b).

Chapter Three
"El licenciado Vidriera,"
or "La historia de un fracaso"

1. I have in progress another book-length manuscript that studies the *novelas* from a formalistic point of view and underscores their narrative features.

2. Pedro de Valencia (1608) also expressed a negative attitude toward the peasant class: " 'Nowadays every farmer, trader, cobbler, blacksmith and plasterer, each of whom love their sons with indiscreet affection, wish to remove them from work and seek for them a more glamorous career. Toward this end, they put them to study. And being students, they learn little but they become delicate and presumptuous. Consequently, they remain without a trade or are made into sacristans or scribes' " (cited by Kagan, *Stud.* 43–44).

3. See Jean-Marc Pelorson's excellent *Les "Letrados": Juristes castillans sous Philippe III (Recherches sur leur place dans la société, la culture et l'état)*. See also Márquez Villanueva's review article "Letrados, consejeros y justicias."

4. "For commoners, the lower nobility, and even for the landless sons of the aristocracy, law was *the* [Kagan's emphasis] road to wealth, influence, and social prestige" (Kagan, *Stud.* xxii). This category would fit Rodaja as not only a commoner but probably as a poor farmer and may clarify his choice of study.

5. See also his comment "No parece ser que estas instituciones ejercieran, como corporación, gran influencia en esta época; pero al mismo tiempo la multiplicación de las Universidades se debía a la urgente demanda que reyes y magnates hacían de hombres educados capaces de coger las riendas del gobierno, especialmente de juristas, cuyo poder e importancia iba en aumento y cuyas Facultades gozaban de los máximos honores" (Jiménez 121).

6. The *colegios mayores*, according to Domínguez Ortiz, were establisted by powerful graduates, in part "for the purpose of helping poor students in the higher branches of learning" (*Golden Age* 233).

7. While it is true that there were extra costs, there were some advantages that students enjoyed, e.g., they were exempt from certain taxes affecting them and their goods (Defourneaux 165).

8. See Addy: "The students who had to get their education and their living outside this charmed circle were resentful, and their resentment was deepened by the haughty conduct of collegians" (60).

9. Addy says: "This system of selection and payment of professors had one other result of great importance; it served to create great resentment and bitterness in the *manteistas* who were not collegians or members of influential religious orders. Barred from the charmed circle of influence, they had difficulty in getting jobs whether in the University, the church, or the government, and their already sensitive feelings were often harried by the haughty and discourteous conduct of their rivals" (24).

10. Parker points out that wealth and position were necessary to reach the heights of a position. He notes that it was only a social and financial elite that could aspire to such positions because oftentimes one had to depend on one's own financial means to carry out responsibilities; this

Notes to Pages 78–89

was especially true for the military. Without personal wealth one had to resign oneself to reaching a certain point and progressing no further (119).

11. While it is generally accepted now that many of Fray Luis's difficulties were brought about by rivalries and professional jealousies among the various religious orders, his *converso* background intensified some of his problems.

12. Erasmus's refusal to come to Spain is well known. But what is less well known is that one of his reasons was that he considered Spain "a land full of Jews." Domínguez Ortiz wonders if Erasmus's attitudes came about through his contacts with the *converso* Juan Luis Vives (*Golden Age* 223).

13. See also Kagan, *Law* 76, for the bad opinion of lawyers because of the *converso* element.

14. While it is true that the crown banned lawyers from Peru, the *cédula* never took effect (see Lockhart, *Spanish Peru* passim). Such a ban was really wishful, indeed Utopian, thinking on the part of the crown, as Kagan suggests in a personal communication.

15. Rodaja's "humble origins" might accord with Castro's assertion that poor *labradores* had less to worry about than educated courtiers when it came to *pureza de sangre* (citing the case of Sancho Panza in *Don Quijote*). Rodaja's poor, country status might point to a non-*converso* life. However, as I stated above (taking support from Kagan, *Law* 71n186) the resourcefulness of *conversos* in entering the legal profession was well known and documented; in which case, Rodaja could still have been of *converso* stock.

16. Forcione asserts that the satire is ambiguous (262); that Cervantes apparently had a low opinion of the satirical genre (283); that Cervantes sees the possibility of natural wisdom and possible reconciliation of satire with Christian principles; that the Christian principles would unite with the satire of light, i.e., uniting Diogenes with Christ.

17. See Johnson's interesting book (*Madness and Lust*) on the psychological and psychoanalytical aspects of *Don Quijote,* which provides a serious view of Quijote's mental aberrations. See also Huarte de San Juan, whom Johnson also quotes.

18. *Diagnostic Statistical Manual,* 3R. I wish to express my thanks to my colleague, Dr. Arthur Rosenkrantz, for helpful information regarding some clinical aspects of Vidriera.

19. Amezúa notes that critics such as Menéndez Pelayo, Icaza, and Alonso Cortés regarded Vidriera's dementia as "una figura adventicia y secundaria, alegando que Cervantes la imaginó para poner en su boca los apotegmas, sentencias y dichos ingeniosos que tenía ya escritos y pensados" (2: 173).

20. Forcione refers to Erasmus's use of the Pauline suggestions (253–54).

21. See also Maravall, who cites as a possible source the *Speculum vitae humanae* of the Bishop Sánchez de Arévalo. He mentions it with respect to the satirical impulse and the observation of society (383).

Rodríguez Luis quotes Avalle-Arce, who sees the glass as a manner of helping us see through things (1: 205).

22. See also Forcione passim, for a good review of that type of literature in the Renaissance.

23. I reject any argument that links this metamorphosis with "real" instances of this kind of obsession; e.g., Gaspar Barth; see Amezúa 2: 154 on this point.

24. Later in the tale it is a priest who cures Vidriera of his derangement. For me, the agent of his cure should not necessarily mean that the solution to his woes is religious in nature. Once again, I interpret the detail of the medicative priest (and the laudatory trip to the Vatican) as an aspect of Cervantes's paying of lip service to the Church and to social decorum, which I believe he has done in other tales and, in a more hidden way, in the prologue of *Las novelas ejemplares*.

25. Rodríguez Luis correctly views the dominant theme of the tale as the intellect of the student type (1: 193). Forcione views Vidriera as "a hopelessly flawed man of the intellect" (314). Vidriera in my view is not the culprit. It is the society that is instead flawed; therefore, a "rational" treatment and relation to that society is out of place. Cervantes seems to be saying that it can only be dealt with englobed in the witty, fork-tongued sayings of a demented person. Forcione also notes that Vidriera becomes the true wise man in his state (314). Having seen the breakdown of reason and balance, it is difficult to judge what constitutes a "true" concept, and this is entirely Cervantine. Forcione is correct in seeing Licenciado Vidriera as a Renaissance man concerned with the problem of knowledge (and we add, learning) and that this is Cervantes's more focused investigation of the problem of knowledge (305): but here again, it is learning that is also being tested. See also Forcione's view of Licenciado Vidriera in isolation as a "powerful symbol of superhuman intelligence, uncompromising rationality, isolated hyper-intellectuality, overly developed sensitivity, and life-denying spirituality" (243); all of which correctly poises the character for an emotional fall.

26. Forcione uses the word *spectacle* with respect to this part of the tale, but he is referring to the parade of people and their vices (271).

27. See Russell 47–58. See also Rodríguez Luis 1: 195, who rejects the notion of "armas y letras." See also Kagan, *Stud.* 32–36, for very useful notes on the subject of "armas y letras." He also observes that "'Armas y letras . . .' became fashionable ornaments for a grandee to display, and the rather lackadaisical crusades in Granada and North Africa afforded ample opportunities to cultivate both" (35). Although his service is not to be confused with the military service of the nobility, which may have been done out of a sense of *noblesse oblige*, Tomás Rueda's service *completes* the cycle of *letras* to *armas*, making of him the more complete—and more symbolic—Renaissance man.

28. The situation of Rueda in military life is full of questions and ironies. He earlier rejects Capitán Valdivia's request that he join the troops for the tour of Europe, yet he ends his life as a soldier. As a student he was exempt from military service (Defourneaux 165), yet his economic necessity may have forced him into it. The narrator's words concerning the difficulties and stresses of the military life were not without their truth in reality. See Parker's chapter entitled "Life in the Army of Flanders" 158–84; especially 183: "The soldier was certainly in constant danger and almost constant discomfort."

29. See Altamira, who underscores the religious nature of the uprising as well as Philip II's heavy repression of it (81, 83).

30. "Spanish historians have not been attracted to study a war which caused the prolonged sacrifice of men, money and prestige, and produced only humiliation, impoverishment and defeat" (Parker x). Parker adds, "Hapsburg Spain was by no means the last imperial power to court ruin by waging a war abroad which it could not manage to win but could not bear to abandon" (xi).

31. One should recall that the war in the Low Countries was not the only military involvement of the nation: "This sustained effort to fight two wars [Armada] simultaneously was a crippling financial burden" (Parker 233). "Spain could find no escape from this deadlock. Peace without total victory was ideologically unacceptable; total victory was militarily impossible" (Parker 136).

Chapter Four
The Prose of Honor

1. Her father would say later, "Y advierte, hija, que más lastima una onza de deshonra pública que una arroba de infamia secreta" (2: 84).

2. The narrator will later refer to Rodolfo as "[el] salteador y robador de su [Leocadia's] honra" (2: 83).

3. Van Beysterveldt posits two equations on the theme of *honra:* "honra-virtud" and "honor-opinión." The former "préférence qui, au Siècle d'or, était le signe distinctif d'appartenance à une élite d'orientation humaniste et qui s'opposait diamétralement à la conception plus plébéienne de l'*honor-opinión*. Dans la première conception l'honneur s'appuie sur les mérites personnels, indépendamment de ce que le monde dit de la valeur de la personne"(22). For Van Beysterveldt, Cervantes belonged to the group of *honra-virtud*. See also Van Beysterveldt 169. Bryson also notes that the code of honor is based on an identification of honor with valor and justice, which is close to the *honra-virtud* equation (7).

4. Menéndez Pidal found Cervantes's particularly individual treatment of the honor theme mentioned in the work of Adolfo de Castro, Rubio, and Américo Castro: "señalaron cada uno por su parte la opinión de Cervantes en discrepancia con el honor" ("Del honor" 170). See also Américo Castro: "Es desde luego significativo que, en asuntos de honra, Cervantes no siga las tendencias habituales (muerte de la adúltera, por ejemplo); su posición respecto de la vida española es sin duda periférica"

("El drama de la honra" 211n4bis). Tómov also points to Cervantes's individual approach to soluciones: "Lope adhiere a la política oficial y escribe la *Dragontea* contra Francis Drake; él piensa que las torturas de los indios son algo legítimo, insigne, cristiano y preside sosegadamente un auto de fe de herejes. Cervantes propende al perdón y cree en la bondad y en la libertad de conciencia" (622). Van Beysterveldt underscores how Juan Ruiz de Alarcón tends toward humanized situations: "D'autre part, la modération dans les vengeances et la préférence de ses personnages à faire prévaloir, en cas d'offense, l'attitude rationnelle sur l'impulsion d'avoir recours à la violence, révèlent la louable intention d'Alarcón d'humaniser les normes sociales, souvent cruelles, découlant du code de l'honneur de l'époque" (78). Surely, Cervantes must be considered among such a group.

5. See above note 3; see also Van Beysterveldt (78). Surely we must count Cervantes among such "cultos" who preferred reason over violence.

6. I cite here a thought of Américo Castro that illustrates perfectly this play between reader and work of art: "'Los libros (para el hombre del siglo de oro) son lo que de ellos es vivido por cada lector. La literatura se personaliza y el vivir individual hace sentir su posible dimensión poética'" (cited in Van Beysterveldt 48).

7. As the reader becomes aware, both in drama and in Cervantes's stories, the guardian of a woman's honor may be the brother. For a comprehensive discussion of the responsibilities surrounding various members of the family on a question of *honra,* see Van Beysterveldt.

8. Ciavarelli says: "Don Rafael, a diferencia de los héroes típicos de los dramas de honor, no se deja llevar por la pasión tradicional que impulsa súbitas reacciones. El héroe cervantino, se vale, en cambio, del magnífico don de la discreción, ya notado y alabado por su incógnita hermana" (191). Menéndez Pidal points out that seventeenth-century drama is largely responsible for taking the notion of "venganza" and applying it to the area of marriage ("Del honor" 166). However, as he also notes, it is the *novela* tradition that will offer a protest to the "venganza de honor": "La novela, pues, y no el teatro, es campo apropiado para protestas contra la venganza de honor" ("Del honor" 171). See the equation that Van Beysterveldt proposes of *honor-virtud* in Cervantes's *novelas* and in his *Quijote.* See Van Beysterveldt 203: "Or, dans la conception de l'honneur qui domine dans le théâtre classique espagnol, l'efficacité de l' 'honor-virtud' est niée."

9. There are of course other comments, direct and indirect, on the question of *honra* in other *novelas,* but I have chosen these because they involve the polemic with Lopean dramaturgy on the subject. In the chapter dealing with "La gitanilla," I discuss the honor question in depth in another context, but I have not included it in this chapter.

10. As a part of the latent subtext that we have seen in other chapters, Cervantes is postulating a background to Carrizales that the average Spanish reader could not ignore. His wealth, which is demonstrated in the tale, can also, as an historical and sociological datum, create suspicions

—e.g., "Le seul fait d'être riche éveillait ainsi des soupçons que la personne en question n'était pas tout à fait de *sangre limpia*" (Van Beysterveldt 189). In this way, Cervantes is juxtaposing the *limpieza* motif with the anti-*limpieza* suspicion, deconstructing his own first-level presentation. If we follow Van Beysterveldt, we must acknowledge his observation that in the theater of the Siglo de Oro, heroines were well dressed and therefore they would be associated with "cristianas viejas" (85–86).

11. See Van Beysterveldt, who focuses on the tendency to keep females isolated from their own social reality. Bearing in mind María de Zayas's *La fuerza del amor,* he quotes Laura: "Et Laura conclut: 'y así, por tenernos sujetas desde que nacemos vais enflaqueciendo nuestras fuerzas con los temores de la honra, y el entendimiento con el recato de la vergüenza, dándonos por espada ruecas, y por libros almohadillas'" (128). Van Beysterveldt continues, "Le fait de tenir la femme à l'écart de la vie publique constituait ainsi dans la société espagnole, dominée par l'idée de l'honneur, une précaution généralement répandue, mais non point généralement admise, pour conserver la vertu de la femme" (128), to which he answers, "A ce sujet, Mlle. del Pilar Oñate dit: 'En la época de Cervantes, como varios siglos después todavía, era creencia general, que en España llegaba a categoría de dogma, que para conservar la virtud de las mujeres, el mejor medio era mantenerlas rigurosamente recluídas en el hogar'" (128). Essentially, Van Beysterveldt believes that it is Cervantes's conception to have females guard their own honor (139). Cf. Sancho Panza's judgment while governor regarding the defense of a woman's honor.

12. The duenna's sarcastic response is quite similar to sentiments found in other genres and works of the Golden Age. It should not surprise us that Cervantes, especially on the subject of *honra,* would have a character enunciate impatience with the concept.

13. This seemingly insignificant detail (Carrizales's not having a weapon with which to murder his wife and Loaysa) is not without some intertexuality. See Mateo Alemán's story of Dorida and Bonifacio. When the fire starts, the lovers are sent out into the street naked. The lieutenant has no way to defend himself.

14. Studying a medieval case of *honra,* Menéndez Pidal says: "la mató, dice el cronista, y no tuvo piedad de ella, olvidando, que Cristo perdonó a la mujer adúltera" ("Del honor" 172). Cervantes has not forgotten, to judge from Carrizales's resolution. His faint and ill-health are not an answer as to why he does not kill both Leonora and Loaysa; a more likely answer is that he believes that such solutions are not sound and certainly are not Christian. Cervantes with this ending is rejecting the notion that vengeance is a form of heroism (see Menéndez Pidal, "Del honor" 162). He is even rejecting the Aristotelian idea that retaliation is a positive trait: Bryson quotes Aristotle: "'It is nobler . . . to avenge ourselves upon our enemies instead of making up quarrels with them; partly because retaliation is just and just conduct is noble, and partly because a brave man should never be beaten. Victory and honor may both be reckoned as noble; for they are desirable in spite of their unproductiveness and are evidences of superiority in virtue'" (44).

Chapter Five
Apologia pro patria sua:
Cervantes's "La señora Cornelia"

1. See Rodríguez Luis, for whom this *novela* is the best example of the Italianate genre (1: 87); he also notes that the characters, being *hidalgos* and in the same social class, are reminiscent of Bandello (1: 87). Rodríguez Luis notes the use of Italian words (1: 87–88n2) but also that the plot, names of characters, political machinations, intervention of *segundones* of the families, some linguistic touches, the use of "casualidades" and "coincidencias," and the "tono peculiar" of the *novelas* all associate this *novela* with the Italianate tradition. Amezúa also sees "La señora Cornelia" as belonging to the "*manera italiana* de Cervantes" (2: 356; Amezúa's emphasis). He sees the action of the *novela* as a part of life: "Las novelas italianas abundan sobremanera en casos semejantes" (2: 370).

2. For El Saffar, it is the influence of the Greek novel, the contemporary *comedia,* and the *Persiles* that offers the source of this *novela* (*Novel to Romance* 119), and the use of "recognition and peripety" and "Cervantes's exploitation of a literary technique much discussed by literary theorists and used by playwrights and imitators of Heliodorus" (127).

3. See Espinosa's fundamental study "El estudiante en el cuento tradicional."

4. See Schiaffino 20, for literary as well as historical associations with Cervantes's work.

5. Astrana Marín gives a very exhaustive and mannered summary of the Italian experience of Cervantes; similar treatments are to be found in Byron (101) and Granados (1–20).

6. See also his "Quant aux descriptions des villes italiennes qui sont un des ornements du *Licencié de Verre,* elles n'expriment pas à l'état brut les préférences du voyage curieux; ce sont le plus souvent des morceaux de bravoure, conformes aux canons de la rhétorique du temps" (Canavaggio 75).

7. See above, chapter 4, "The Prose of Honor." Here I will only deal with the problem of rival nationalities as they are reflected in this *novela.*

8. With respect to Spanish literature and Spanish books, Croce says, "Questo brano del Lando conferma che i libri spagnuoli in genere ebbero bensí voga e suscitarono talvolta persino fanatismo, ma, come tutte le altre galanterie e pompe e cerimonie e raffinatezze e sottigliezze introdotte dagli spagnuoli, furono quanto efficaci del costume di certe classi sociali, altretanto sterili di efficacia sulla vita del pensiero e dell'arte, innanzi alla quale splendevano allora, in Italia, ben altri modelli e ideali" (180).

9. See Louis Imperiale's book on *La lozana andaluza,* which studies the "Spanish world" of Rome; he also has a forthcoming book on Delicado and Aretino.

10. "Nelle divise d'amore, nelle vesti e livree con molti allusivi, essi, insieme coi francesi e più dei francesi, furono maestri e modelli agli italiani" (Croce 185).

11. For the *libros de caballerías* as consistent with a Counter-Reformation view, see Bryant L. Creel, *Don Quijote, Symbol of a Culture in Crisis.*

12. See Croce (28), who refers to Masuccio's fortieth *novella* for support of this idea.

13. The text is even more explicit, as when the *ama* says, "El señor Lorenzo, italiano, y que se fíe de españoles" (2: 262).

14. Further evidence of Cervantes's manipulation of a situation to his end of presenting the Spanish culture in a good light can be seen at the dinner scene. El Saffar comments, "The final dinner brings the characters together not only along familial lines, but along international and social lines" (*Novel to Romance* 124). Casalduero utters a similar thought that reflects the positive joining of two cultures in "La señora Cornelia," "Sobre un fondo de hidalguía española—dignidad, religiosidad, valor, nobleza, generosidad—, la atrayente vida italiana—soportales de mármol, noche de aventuras, chocar de espadas" (179).

15. See Croce 36, 80, 92, 96, 99, respectively.

16. Cf. Croce: "E, in effetti, verso la metà del secolo Napoli sembrava già, quanto a lingua, un paese mezzo spagnuolo" (158).

17. Also the Zúñiga, Requensen, and Revertera families; see Croce 234.

18. See also Don Juan, who says, "y tomo a mi cargo la satisfac[c]ión o venganza de vuestro agravio; y esto no sólo por ser español, sino por ser caballero y serlo vos tan principal" (2: 258).

19. Concerning Spanish nobility, El Saffar notes that "Don Juan and don Antonio represent the ideal of the young Spanish gentleman. They are noble, devoted, generous, courageous, and given to a thirst for both learning and adventure. Their perfection and balance contrast sharply with the overly cerebral and self-seeking major characters of Cervantes's earlier fiction" (*Novel to Romance* 121).

20. Perhaps it would be wise to recall Casalduero's predilection for a spiritual and religious view of the *novelas*. We must then recognize here Cervantes's wish to paint the portrait of the perfect Spanish nobleman and his religious piety, which in that era could not be omitted from such a portrait.

21. There are other Italian language references in the *novela*. (See Rodríguez Luis 1: 87–88n2 for a list of these.)

22. He even notes the use of Spanish in a rather special situation "ove un cavagliero che sia stato quattro giorni a Spagna vole che se creda che egli si sia scordato il parlare natio, e che quasi a forza le parole e frasi spagnuole gli corrino in bocca" (Croce 159).

Selected Bibliography

Addy, George M. *The Enlightenment in the University of Salamanca.* Durham, NC: Duke UP, 1966.

Altamira, Rafael. *Historia de España y de la civilización española.* Vol. 3. Barcelona: Gili, 1913.

Alter, Robert. *Partial Magic: The Novel as a Self-Conscious Genre.* Berkeley and Los Angeles: U of California P, 1975.

Amezúa. See González de Amezúa y Mayo, Agustín de.

Andrews, Kenneth R. *Elizabethan Privateering; English Privateering during the Spanish War, 1585–1603.* Cambridge: UP, 1964.

Apráiz y Sáenz del Burgo, Julián. *Estudio histórico-crítico sobre las 'Novelas ejemplares' de Cervantes.* Vitoria: Domingo Sar, 1901.

Astrana Marín, Luis. *Cervantes y otros ensayos.* Madrid: Aguado, 1944.

———. *Vida ejemplar y heroica de Miguel de Cervantes Saavedra.* Vol. 2. Madrid: Reus, 1949.

Avalle-Arce, Juan Bautista. "Lope de Vega and Cervantes." *Texas Quarterly* 6.1 (1963): 190–202.

Aylward, Edward. *Cervantes, Pioneer and Plagiarist.* London: Tamesis, 1982.

Bataillon, Marcel. "Cervantès et 'le mariage chrétien.'" *Bulletin Hispanique* 49.2 (1947): 129–44. Rpt. as "Cervantes y 'el matrimonio cristiano'" in his *Varia lección de clásicos españoles.* Madrid: Gredos, 1964. 238–55.

Bible, The New Oxford Annotated, with the Apocrypha. Revised Standard Version. Ed. Herbert G. May and Bruce M. Metzger. New York: Oxford UP, 1973, 1977.

Blanco Aguinaga, Carlos. "Cervantes y la picaresca: notas sobre dos tipos de realismo." *Nueva Revista de Filología Hispánica* 11 (1957): 313–42.

Bleiberg, Germán. *Diccionario de historia de España.* 2nd ed. Vol. 3. Madrid: Revista de Occidente, 1969.

Brookes, Kristen G. "Readers, Authors and Characters in *Don Quijote.*" *Cervantes* 12 (1992): 73–92.

Brownlee, Marina S. *The Poetics of Literary Theory: "Novelas a Marcia Leonarda" and Their Cervantine Context.* Potomac, MD: Studia Humanitatis, 1981.

Bryson, Frederick R. *The Point of Honor in Sixteenth Century Italy: An Aspect of the Life of a Gentleman.* Chicago: U of Chicago, 1935.

Selected Bibliography

Byron, William. *Cervantes: A Biography.* Garden City, NY: Doubleday, 1978.

Campbell, Kenneth L. *The Intellectual Struggle of the English Papists in the Seventeenth Century (The Catholic Dilemma).* Texas Studies in Religion 30. Lewiston/Queenston: Mellen, 1986.

Canavaggio, Jean. *Cervantès.* Paris: Mazarines, 1986.

Caro Baroja, Julio. "Honour and Shame: A Historical Account of Several Conflicts." *Honour and Shame: The Values of Mediterranean Society.* Ed. Jean G. Peristiany. Chicago: U of Chicago P, 1966. 81–137.

———. Epilogue/Prologue. "Los gitanos en la literatura española." Clébert 278–312.

Casalduero, Joaquín. *Sentido y forma de las novelas ejemplares.* Buenos Aires: Instituto de Filología, 1943.

Castro, Américo. "El celoso extremeño de Cervantes." *Semblanzas y estudios españoles.* Princeton: privately printed, 1956. 271–95.

———. "El drama de la honra en España y en su literatura." *De la edad conflictiva.* Vol. 1. Madrid: Taurus, 1961.

———. "La ejemplaridad de las novelas cervantinas." *Semblanzas y estudios españoles.* Princeton: privately printed, 1956. 297–315.

Cervantes Saavedra, Miguel de. *Las novelas ejemplares.* Ed. H. Sieber. 2 vols. Madrid: Cátedra, 1982.

———. *El ingenioso hidalgo Don Quijote de la Mancha.* 2 vols. Ed. John J. Allen. Madrid: Cátedra, 1977.

Chacón y Calvo, José María. "El realismo ideal de *La gitanilla.*" *Boletín de la Academia Cubana de la Lengua* 2 (1953): 246–67.

Ciavarelli, Maria Elisa. *El tema de la fuerza de la sangre.* Madrid: Porrúa Turanzas, 1980.

Clébert, Jean-Paul. *Los gitanos.* Trans. Carmen Alcalde and María Rosa Prats. Barcelona: Aymá, 1965. Trans. of *Les Tziganes.*

Coello, Antonio. *El conde de Sex.* Critical ed. and study by Donald E. Schmiedel. Madrid: Playor, 1973.

Colie, Rosalie. *The Resources of Kind: Genre Theory in the Renaissance.* Ed. B. K. Lewalski. Berkeley and Los Angeles: U of California P, 1973.

Covarrubias, Sebastián de. *Tesoro de la lengua castellana o española.* Madrid: Turner, 1979.

Creel, Byrant L. *Don Quijote, Symbol of a Culture in Crisis.* Valencia: Albatros Hispanófila, 1988.

Croce, Benedetto. *La Spagna nella vita italiana durante la Rinascenza.* Bari: Laterza, 1949.

Selected Bibliography

D'Antuono, Nancy. *Boccaccio's "Novelle" in the Theater of Lope de Vega*. Potomac, MD: Studia Humanitatis, 1983.

Defourneaux, Marcelin. *Daily Life in Spain in the Golden Age*. Trans. N. Branch. New York: Praeger, 1970, 1971.

Diagnostic Statistical Manual, 3R. Washington, DC: APA, 1987.

Domínguez Ortiz, Antonio. "Documentación sobre los gitanos españoles en el siglo XVII." *Homenaje a Julio Caro Baroja*. Ed. Carreira, Cid, Gutiérrez Esteve, Rubio. Madrid: Centro de Investigaciones Sociológicas, 1978. 319–26.

———. *The Golden Age of Spain, 1516–1659*. Trans. James Casey. New York: Basic Books, 1971.

Dunn, Peter N. "Las 'Novelas ejemplares.'" *Suma cervantina*. Ed. J. B. Avalle-Arce and E. C. Riley. London: Tamesis, 1973.

Durán, Manuel. *Cervantes*. New York: Twayne, 1974.

El Saffar, Ruth. *Distance and Control in Don Quixote; A Study in Narrative Technique*. Studies in the Romance Languages and Literatures 147. Chapel Hill: U of North Carolina P, Dept. of Romance Languages, 1975.

———. *Novel to Romance: A Study of Cervantes's "Novelas ejemplares."* Baltimore: Johns Hopkins UP, 1974.

Espinosa, Aurelio. "El estudiante en el cuento tradicional." *Estudios dedicados a Menéndez Pidal*. Vol. 3. Madrid: C.S.I.C., 1952. 247–64.

Fernández Santamaría, José Antonio. *The State, War, and Peace: Spanish Political Thought in the Renaissance 1516–79*. London: Cambridge UP, 1977.

Finello, Dominick L. *Pastoral Themes and Forms in Cervantes's Fiction*. Lewisburg, PA: Bucknell UP, Associated U Presses, 1994.

Fontes, Manuel da Costa. "Love as an Equalizer in *La española inglesa*." *Romance Notes* 16.3 (1975): 1–7.

Forcione, Alban K. *Cervantes and the Humanist Vision: A Study of Four Exemplary Novels*. Princeton: Princeton UP, 1982.

García Gómez, Angel M. "Una historia sefardí como posible fuente de *La española inglesa* de Cervantes." *Actas del segundo coloquio internacional de la asociación de Cervantistas*. Madrid: Anthropos, 1991. 621–28.

García Mercadal, José. *Estudiantes, sopistas, pícaros*. Madrid: Plutarco, 1934.

Gerli, Michael. "Idealism and Irony in *La gitanilla*." *Cervantes* 6.1 (Spring 1986): 29–36.

Selected Bibliography

González de Amezúa y Mayo, Agustín de. *Cervantes: creador de la novela corta española.* 2 vols. Madrid: C.S.I.C., 1956.

Granados, Juana. *Motivi e ricordi d'Italia nell'opera cervantina.* Milano: La Goliardica, 1960.

Grande, Félix. "Los gitanos: una mirada sobre nuestra memoria." *Raíces (Revista Judía de Cultura)* 2 (1986): 27–29.

———. *Memoria del flamenco.* Introd. José Manuel Caballero Bonald. 2 vols. Madrid: Espasa-Calpe, 1979.

Greenblatt, Stephen J. *Renaissance Self-Fashioning: from More to Shakespeare.* Chicago: U of Chicago P, 1980.

Hart, Thomas. *Cervantes' Exemplary Fictions: A Study of the "Novelas Ejemplares."* Lexington, KY: UP of Kentucky, 1994.

Holmes, Peter. *Resistance and Compromise: The Political Thought of the Elizabethan Catholics.* Cambridge: Cambridge UP, 1982.

Huarte [de San Juan], Juan. *Examen de ingenios: The Examination of Mens Wits (1594).* Gainesville, FL: Scholars' Facsimiles and Reprints, 1959.

Icaza, Francisco A. de. *Las novelas ejemplares de Cervantes: sus críticos, sus modelos literarios.* Madrid: Ateneo de Madrid, 1916.

Imperiale, Louis. *El contexto dramático de "La lozana andaluza."* Potomac, MD: Scripta Humanistica, 1991.

Janson, Horst Waldemar. *History of Art.* Englewood Cliffs, NJ: Prentice-Hall, 1986.

Jiménez, Alberto. *Historia de la universidad española.* Madrid: Alianza, 1971.

Johnson, Carroll B. "'La española inglesa' and the Practice of Literary Production." *Viator* 19 (1988): 377–416.

———. *Madness and Lust: A Psychoanalytical Approach to Don Quijote.* Berkeley and Los Angeles: U of California P, 1983.

Kagan, Richard. *Lawsuits and Litigation in Castile 1500–1700.* Chapel Hill: U of North Carolina P, 1981.

———. *Students and Society in Early Modern Spain.* Baltimore: Johns Hopkins UP, 1974.

Kamen, Henry. *The Spanish Inquisition.* New York: New American Library, 1965.

Larson, Donald N. *The Honor Plays of Lope de Vega.* Cambridge: Harvard UP, 1977.

Laspéras, Jean-Michel. *La Nouvelle en Espagne au Siècle d'Or.* Montpellier: Castillet, 1987.

Selected Bibliography

Leblon, Bernard. *Les Gitans de la littérature espagnole.* Toulouse-Le Mirail: Institut d'Etudes Hispaniques et Hispano-Américaines, Université de Toulouse-Le Mirail, 1982.

———. *Les Gitans d'Espagne: Le Prix de la différence.* Paris: PUF, 1985.

Lockhart, James M. *Spanish Peru, 1532–1560: A Colonial Society.* Madison: U of Wisconsin P, 1968.

López Rodríguez, Manuel. *Tras las huellas del flamenco.* Jérez de la Frontera: Cátedra de Flamencología, 1971.

Lowe, Jennifer. *Two Novelas ejemplares (La gitanilla and La ilustre fregona).* London: Grant, Cutler/Tamesis, 1971.

Maravall, Juan Antonio. "'Los hombres de saber' o letrados y la formación de su conciencia estamental." *Estudios de historia del pensamiento español.* Ser. 1, Edad Media. 2a. ed. ampliada. Madrid: Cultura Hispánica, 1973. 355–89.

Mariana, Juan de. "Tratado contra los juegos públicos." *Obras completas.* By Mariana. Vol. 2. Biblioteca de autores españoles 31. Madrid: M. Rivadeneyra, 1854.

Márquez Villanueva, Francisco. "La buenaventura de Preciosa." *Nueva Revista de Filología Hispánica* 34.2 (1985–86): 745–68.

———. "Letrados, consejeros y justicias." Rev. of *Les 'Letrados': Juristes castillans sous Philippe III (Recherches sur leur place dans la société, la culture et l'état)*, by J.-M. Pelorson. *Hispanic Review* 53.2 (1985): 201–27.

———. Rev. of *Cervantes and the Humanist Vision*, by A. K. Forcione. *Cervantes* 4.2 (1984): 123–37.

Mattingly, Garrett. *The Defeat of the Spanish Armada.* Boston: Houghton, 1984.

Menéndez Pidal, Ramón. "Del honor en el teatro español." *De Cervantes a Lope de Vega.* Buenos Aires/México: Espasa-Calpe, 1940. 153–84.

———, ed. *Primera crónica general de España.* By Alfonso X. 2 vols. Fuentes cronísticas de la historia de España 1. 3d ed. Madrid: Gredos, 1977.

Moncada, Sancho de. *Restauración política de España.* Ed. Jean Vilar Berrogain. Clásicos de pensamiento económico español. Madrid: Inst. de Estudios Fiscales, Ministerio de Hacienda, 1974.

Montrose, Louis A. "The Elizabethan Subject and the Spenserian Text." *Literary Theory/Renaissance Texts.* Ed. Patricia A. Parker and David Quint. Baltimore: Johns Hopkins UP, 1986.

Morey, Adrian. *The Catholic Subjects of Elizabeth I.* Totawa, NJ: Rowman and Littlefield, 1978.

Selected Bibliography

Norman, Edward R. *Roman Catholicism in England from the Elizabethan Settlement to the Second Vatican Council.* Oxford: UP, 1985.

Northup, George T., ed. *Three Plays by Calderón.* Boston/New York: Heath, 1926.

Parker, Geoffrey. *The Army of Flanders and the Spanish Road, 1567–1659: The Logistics of Spanish Victory and Defeat in the Low Countries' Wars.* Cambridge: Cambridge UP, 1972.

Parr, James A. *Don Quijote: An Anatomy of Subversive Discourse.* Newark, DE: Juan de la Cuesta Monograph Series, 1988.

Pelorson, Jean-Marc. *Les "Letrados": Juristes castillans sous Philippe III (Recherches sur leur place dans la société, la culture et l'état).* N.p.: n.p., with l'Université de Poitiers, 1980 (Le Puy-en-Velay: L'Eveil de la Haute-Loire, 1980).

Peristiany, Jean G. "Honour and Shame." *Honour and Shame: The Values of Mediterranean Society.* Ed. Peristiany. Chicago: U of Chicago P, 1966.

Piel, Joseph M., and Dieter Kremer. *Hispano-gotisches Namenbuch.* Heidelberg: Winter Universitätsverlag, 1976.

Pierce, Frank. "Reality and Realism in the Exemplary Novels." *Bulletin of Hispanic Studies* 30.119 (1953): 134–42.

Pitt-Rivers, Julian. "Honour and Social Status." *Honour and Shame: The Values of Mediterranean Society.* Ed. Jean G. Peristiany. Chicago: U of Chicago P, 1966. 19–77.

Plowden, Alison. *Danger to Elizabeth; the Catholics under Elizabeth I.* London: Macmillan, 1973.

Rauhut, Franz. "Consideraciones sociológicas sobre 'La gitanilla.'" *Anales cervantinos* 3 (1953): 145–60.

Ricapito, Joseph V. "Cervantes and the Picaresque: Redivivo." *Hispanic Studies in Honor of Joseph H. Silverman.* Ed. Ricapito. Newark, DE: Juan de la Cuesta Hispanic Monographs Series, 1988. 319–43.

———. "Cervantes y Mateo Alemán: de nuevo." *Anales Cervantinos* 23 (1985): 91–95. (Published in 1988.)

———. "La estructura del *Guzmán de Alfarache* de Mateo Alemán." *Ibero-Romania* ns, no. 21 (1985): 48–64.

Ricart, Domingo. "El concepto de la honra en el teatro del Siglo de Oro y las ideas de Juan de Valdés." *Segismundo* 1 (1985): 43–69.

Rico, Francisco, ed. *Las novelas a Marcia Leonarda.* By Lope de Vega. Madrid: Alianza, 1968.

Riley, Edward C. *Cervantes's Theory of the Novel.* Oxford: Clarendon, 1968.

Selected Bibliography

Rodríguez Luis, Julio. *Novedad y ejemplo de las novelas de Cervantes.* 2 vols. Madrid: Porrúa Turanzas, 1980.

Rosales, Luis. "Cervantes y la libertad." *Insula* no. 64 (15 Apr. 1951): 1, 6-7.

Rotunda, Dominic P. *Motif-Index of the Italian Novelle in Prose.* Folklore Series 2. Bloomington: Indiana UP, 1942.

———. *A Tabulation of Early Italian Tales.* University of California Publications in Modern Philology. Berkeley and Los Angeles: U of California P, 1930.

Russell, Peter. "Arms versus Letters: Toward a Definition of Fifteenth Century Humanism." *Aspects of the Renaissance: A Symposium.* Austin: U of Texas P, 1967.

Sánchez Ortega, María Helena. *Documentación selecta sobre la situación de los gitanos españoles en el siglo XVIII.* Madrid: Nacional, 1976.

Schiaffino, Rafael. *Cervantes y el renacimiento: conferencia pronunciada en la Sociedad Dante Alighiera en Roma, el 20 de julio de 1949.* Montevideo: Revista Nacional, 1950.

Selig, Karl-Ludwig. "Concerning the Structure of Cervantes's *Dead Souls.*" *Romanistisches Jahrbuch* 13 (1992): 273–76.

Sicroff, Albert A. *Les Controverses des statuts de "pureté de sang" en Espagne du XVe au XVIIe Siècle.* Paris: Didier, 1960.

Starkie, Walter. "Cervantes and the Gypsies." *Huntington Library Quarterly* 26.4 (1963): 337–49.

ter Horst, Robert. "Une Saison en enfer—La gitanilla." *Cervantes* 5.2 (1985): 87–127.

Thompson, E. A. *Los godos en España.* Trans. Javier Faci. Madrid: Alianza, 1971. Trans. of *The Goths in Spain.* Oxford: Oxford UP, 1969.

Tómov, Tomás. "Cervantes y Lope de Vega (Un caso de enemistad literaria)." *Actas del segundo congreso internacional de hispanistas.* Ed. J. Sánchez Romeralo and N. Poulussen. Nimega: Instituto Español de la Universidad de Nimega, 1967. 617–26.

Torre, Guillermo de. "El postulante y el favorito (Cervantes y Lope de Vega)." *Atenea* 268 (1947): 41–50.

Van Beysterveldt, Antonie A. *Repercussions du souci de la pureté de sang sur la conception de l'honneur dans la 'comedia' espagnole.* Leiden: Brill, 1966.

Watkin, Edward I. *Roman Catholicism in England from the Reformation to 1950.* London: Oxford UP, 1957.

Selected Bibliography

Weiger, John. *In the Margins of Cervantes.* Hanover: U of Vermont / UP of New England, 1988.

Wilson, Diana DeArmas. "Defending 'Poor Poetry': Sidney, Cervantes and the Prestige of Epic." 2nd Biennial Conference of the Society for Renaissance and Baroque Hispanic Poetry. U of Houston, 17 Nov. 1995.

Index

Acquaviva, Cardinal, 121, 122, 123, 124, 133
Act of Supremacy, 41, 50
Acuña, Don Pedro de, 60
Addy, George M., 75, 79, 143nn8 and 9
Aeneid, 85
Alcalá de Henares, 69, 71, 76, 82, 92
Aldine presses, 125
Alemán, Mateo, 2, 3, 4, 5, 7, 97, 117, 135Intro n2, 148n13
Alfonso el Sabio, 74
Allen, Dr. William, 43, 140n8
Alonso Cortés, Narciso, 89, 144n19
Altamira, Rafael, 60, 142n18, 146n29
Alter, Robert, 135n4
Alvarez Vallejo, Manuel, 139n2
Amadís, 125, 130
Amezúa. *See* González de Amezúa y Mayo, Agustín
Andrews, Kenneth R., 42, 43, 64, 65, 66
Appellants, 51, 52
Aretino, Pietro, 126, 130, 150n9
Arévalo, José Carlos, 15
Ariosto, Ludovico, 124, 129
Aristotle, 86, 103, 148n14
Armada, 18, 39, 42, 56, 57, 61, 62, 63, 141n18
armas y letras, 91, 92, 145n27
Armistead, Samuel G., 7, 142n22
Arróniz, Othón, 103
Astrana Marín, Luis, 128, 149n5
Atkinson, Robert, 51
Audebert, Nicholas, 130
Avalle-Arce, Juan Bautista, 5, 98, 145n21
Aylward, Edward, 140n11

Bandello, 122, 149n1
Barth, Gaspar, 145n23

Bataillon, Marcel, 5, 138n21
Blackwell, Archpriest George, 51
Blanco Aguinaga, Carlos, 135Intro n1
Bleiberg, Germán, 142n23
Boccaccio, Giovanni, 2, 121, 122, 124
Boiardo, Matteo Maria, 124
Bologna, city of, 106, 122
Brookes, Kristen G., 5
Brownlee, Marina S., 103
Bryson, Frederick R., 99, 146n3, 148–49n14
Bull of Excommunication, 50
Buscón, Vida del, 83, 84, 104
Byron, William, 149n5

Cabrera Núñez, Melchor de, 80
Cádiz, battles of, 39, 58, 59, 60, 61, 64, 67, 139n2
Calderón de la Barca, Pedro, 7, 99
caló, 34–35
Campbell, Kenneth L., 40, 41, 49, 58–59, 140n10
Campion, Edmund, 48, 55. *See also* Jesuits
Canavaggio, Jean, 121, 122, 124, 125, 128, 149n6
Carlisle, Bishop of (Owen Oglethorp), 41
Caro Baroja, Julio, 100, 136n9
Carrasco, Sansón, 76
Cartagena, Alfonso de, 130
Casalduero, Joaquín, 5, 7, 27, 29, 42, 56, 81, 88, 89, 91, 92, 123, 124, 139n27, 141n14, 150n14
castellanos nuevos. *See* New Castillians
Castro, Adolfo de, 146n4
Castro, Américo, 5, 6, 99, 108, 116, 117, 135Intro n1, 138n22, 139n25, 144n15, 146–47n4, 147n6

159

Index

Castro y Aguila, Licenciado Tomás, 92
Catholic Kings, 11, 12, 21, 73, 75
Catholics, secret. *See* recusancy
Cecil, Robert, 48
Celestina, 130
Chacón y Calvo, José María, 36
Charles III, 12
Charles IV, 12
Charles V, 11, 61, 75, 135ch1 n1
Ciavarelli, Maria Elisa 104, 147n8
Cisneros, Cardinal, 69
Clébert, Jean-Paul, 16, 18, 19, 20, 22, 25, 28, 30, 31, 136n7
Coello, Antonio, 139n2
Colegio Español, 125
colegios mayores, 71, 73, 75, 76, 79, 143n6
Colie, Rosalie, 104
Colleton, John, 49, 50, 59
conversos, 4, 53, 55, 56, 57, 63, 68, 78, 79, 80, 81, 91, 139n25, 141n17, 144nn11–13 and 15
1 Corinthians, 88
Cortes, 11, 18, 28
Counter-Reformation, 7, 27, 29, 82, 91, 123, 124, 129, 140n9, 150n11
Covarrubias, Sebastián de, 16–17, 19, 34–35, 135ch1 n1, 136n5
Creel, Bryant L., 71, 150n11
cristianos nuevos. *See* New Christians
cristianos viejos. *See* Old Christians
Croce, Benedetto, 1, 122, 124, 125, 126, 127, 129, 130, 133, 149n8, 150nn10 and 12 and 15–17 and 22
Cumberland, Henry, Earl of, 64
Cynics, 86

Dante, 125
Defourneaux, Marcelin, 69, 75–76, 77, 78, 82, 92, 143n7, 146n28
De Docta Ignorantia, 86
De Sensu, 86
de Torre, Guillermo. *See* Torre, Guillermo de
diablo cojuelo, El, 84
Díaz de Fregenal, Vasco, 128
Diogenes, 89, 144n16
Domínguez Ortiz, Antonio, 12–13, 71, 143n6, 144n12
Don Quijote, 2, 3, 34, 76, 84, 92, 97, 106, 135n4
Don Quijote apócrifo, 104
Dorida and Bonifacio, 117, 148n13
Dos Passos, John, 7–8
Downham, Bishop of Chester, 141n12
Dragontea, La, 147n4
Drake, Sir Francis, 39, 43, 59–60, 147n4
Dunn, Peter, 5, 37
Durán, Manuel, 5, 12, 139n27

Ecclesiasticus, 87
Edict of Nantes, 59
education, in sixteenth-century Spain, 69–78. *See also colegios mayores*
Elizabeth I of England, 40, 42, 57, 58, 59, 63–64, 141n16
  and the Armada, 56–57, 60–62, 139–40n3
  and the Gypsies, 12
  and Philip II, 42–43
  and recusancy, 39, 41, 42–47, 50–56, 140n5
El Saffar, Ruth, 5, 32, 78, 89–90, 91, 132, 135n4, 139n24, 149n2, 150nn14 and 19
Encina, Juan del, 130
Enríquez de Guzmán, Don García, 127

160

Index

Erasmus, 7, 9, 82, 86, 144nn12 and 20
Espinosa, Aurelio, 149n3
Essex, Earl of, 40, 42, 60, 139n2
esclava de su galán, La, 116
estamentos, 77

Fernández de Avellaneda, Alonso, 104
Fernández de Moratín, Leandro, 118
Fernández Santamaría, José Antonio, 82
Finello, Dominick, 135n4
Five Mile Act of 1593, 47
Flanders, 72, 92, 93, 94
Fontes, Manuel da Costa, 141n17
Forcione, Alban K., 6, 7, 9, 13, 14, 29, 32, 81, 82, 83, 84, 86, 88–89, 137n13, 139n25, 144nn16 and 20, 145nn22 and 25–26

Garcilaso de la Vega, 125, 130
García Gómez, Angel M., 141n17
García Mercadal, José, 69
Garden of Eden, 91
Geertz, Clifford, 8
Gerli, Michael, 35, 36
Gerónimo, Fray, 108
Giannini, Alfredo, 123
Gibbons, John, 140n8
Gilman, Stephen, 1, 7
Ginés de Pasamonte, 2, 3
Giraldi Cinzio, Giovanni, 127
González de Amezúa y Mayo, Agustín, 5, 26, 81, 84, 93, 123, 127, 131, 144n19, 145n23, 149n1
Granados, Juana, 122, 149n5
Grande, Félix, 12, 15–16, 20, 22, 135ch1 n1
Greek romance, 5, 124
Greenblatt, Stephen, 6, 8–9, 37, 142n19

Guevara, Antonio de, 74
Gunpowder Plot, 48
Guzmán de Alfarache, 2, 3, 4, 83, 84
Gypsies, 11–37

Hapsburgs, 90. *See also* Charles V; Philip II; Philip III
Hart, Thomas, 6
Heliodorus, 34, 149n2
Henry IV of France, 52, 59
Henry VIII of England, 45
Heraclitus, 86
heretics, 29, 40, 46, 51, 54
  Arians, 67
Herodotus, 85
Hesiod, 86
Holmes, Peter, 51, 52, 140nn4–5
Holy See. *See* Pope (Papacy)
honra, 33, 34, 99, 100, 101–03, 104, 106, 108, 109, 110, 111–13, 113–17, 148n12, 148–49n14
Howard, Lord Charles, of Effingham, 40, 60
Huarte de San Juan, Juan, 86, 144n17
Hutchinson, Steven, 6

Icaza, Francisco A. de, 36, 59, 144n19
Imperiale, Louis, 150n9
Inquisition, 20
insurgents, in northern England, 49
Italian attitudes
  toward Spain, 121, 122, 124, 125, 126, 127, 128, 129, 130, 131, 132, 134, 150nn9 and 13
  toward Valencia (and Catalans generally), 127, 129, 130
Italian cities, 123, 130

James I of England, 40, 50, 52, 57–58, 58–59, 140n10

161

Index

Janson, Horst Waldemar, 72
jerigonza, 34–35
Jesuits, 47, 51, 52, 55, 57
Jews, 11, 12, 18, 19–21, 22, 27, 53, 55, 57, 68, 79, 80, 99, 141n14, 144n12
Jiménez, Alberto, 69, 75, 78, 143n5
Johnson, Carroll B., 6, 39, 40, 50, 52–53, 57, 58, 59, 60, 66–67, 86, 139n1, 142nn20 and 21, 144n17
Juvenal, 85

Kagan, Richard, 70, 71, 72, 73, 74, 76, 77, 79, 80, 81, 82, 92, 143nn2 and 4, 144nn13 and 15, 145n27
Kamen, Henry, 69, 76, 77, 79
Kremer, Dieter, 142n22

Laínez, Pedro, 124
Larson, Donald N., 100
Laspéras, Jean-Marc, 29, 138nn16 and 21
Lazarillo de Tormes, 2, 7, 83, 84
Leblon, Bernard, 11, 14, 15, 16, 18, 19, 20, 22, 24–25, 28, 29, 31–32, 34, 135ch1 n1, 136n8, 137n13, 138nn14 and 18–19, 139n24
León, Fray Luis de, 78, 144n11
Leovigildo, 67, 68
Lepanto, Battle of, 59, 62, 63, 64, 68
letrado(s), 71, 72, 74, 76, 143n3
libros de caballerías, 129, 150n11
limpieza de sangre, 34, 79–80, 144n15, 147–48n10
  statutes of, 17, 79–80, 99–100
Lockhart, James M., 144n14
López Rodríguez, Manuel, 37
Louis XIV of France, 12
Lowe, Jennifer, 26–27, 32, 35

lozana andaluza, La, 150n9
Lucian, 85

Macrobius, 85
malsinismo, 55
Manrique, Fray Angel, 70
Maravall, José Antonio, 72, 74, 76, 144n21
Mariana, Father, 13, 31, 32
Marino, Gianbattista, 127
maritime references, 39, 42, 43, 44, 59, 61, 62, 63–66, 67, 141–42n18
Márquez Villanueva, Francisco, 5, 7, 137n11, 143n3
marranos, 54
Martial, 86
Martínez de Recalde, Juan, 61
Martínez Silíceo, Juan Cardinal, 79
Martire, Pietro, 130
Mary Stuart, of Scotland, 50
Mary Tudor, of England, 40, 41
Masuccio, 122
Mattingly, Garrett, 60, 61, 62, 142n18
Medina Sidonia, Duke of, 50, 60, 67
Menéndez Pelayo, Marcelino, 84, 144n19
Menéndez Pidal, Ramón, 5, 6, 103, 109, 116, 142n24, 146n4, 147n8, 148n14
Mendoza, Don Diego di, 126
merchants, 66–67
Molho, Maurice, 6
Moncada, Sancho de, 14–15, 16, 19, 20, 23, 28, 30, 31, 34
Montoya, Juan Manuel, 14
Montrose, Louis, 57, 58, 139–40n3
Moors, 11, 12, 18, 19–22, 22, 27, 28, 53, 68, 99
Morante, Elsa, 7
Moratín. *See* Fernández de Moratín, Leandro

162

Index

Morey, Adrian, 40, 45, 46, 47, 48, 49, 50, 54, 55, 56, 140n9, 141n12

Navagero, Andrea, 130
Navarro, Pedro de, 127
Neale, Sir John Ernest, 47
New Castillians (*castellanos nuevos*), 12, 20, 34, 136n7
New Christians (*cristianos nuevos*), 12, 17, 19, 20, 34, 53, 63, 78, 79, 80, 81, 135–36n3
New Historicism, 8
Nicholas of Cusa, 86
Norman, Edward, 43
Northup, George T., 116
Novelas a Marcia Leonarda, 98, 103
Novísima recopilación, 12, 17, 135ch1 nn1 and 2

Oath of Supremacy, 49
Oglethorp, Owen (Bishop of Carlisle), 41
Old Christians (*cristianos viejos*), 17, 21, 79, 80
Oñate, Mlle. del Pilar, 148n11
Ortega y Gasset, José, 1

Paget, Charles, 52
Parker, Geoffrey, 92, 93, 94, 143–44n10, 146nn28 and 30–31
Parr, James, 5
pasajero, El, 74
patriotism, Spanish, 121, 129, 131, 132, 133, 134, 150n14
Paul (the apostle), 88, 144n20
"Pedro de Urdemalas," 18, 19, 35
Pelorson, Jean-Marc, 143n3
pentimento, 56
Peregrino (by Lope de Vega), 97
Peristiany, Jean G., 100
Persons, Robert, 43, 51–52, 55, 140n8

Petrarch, 124
Philip II, 40, 50, 53, 59, 66, 68, 74, 75, 77, 82–83, 93, 125, 146n29
and the Armada, 61–63
and Elizabeth I of England, 42–43
and Gypsies, 11–12, 135ch1 n2
Philip III, 43, 53, 68, 74, 82, 93
Philip IV, 12, 74
Philip V, 12, 74
picaresque, 4, 83, 139n26
Piel, Joseph M., 142n22
Plácida y Victoriano, 130
Plato, 85
Plowden, Alison, 40, 41, 45, 48, 54, 55, 63, 140n4
Plumtree, Thomas, 49
Pope (Papacy), 40, 42, 43, 44, 45, 46, 50, 56, 59, 124, 126, 134, 141n15, 145n24
Pius V, 41
Portugal, 66
pragmatics, 11, 12, 15, 21, 136n4
Proverbs, Book of, 86–87
Pulgar, Hernando del, 77
pureté de sang. See *limpieza de sangre*
pureza de sangre. See *limpieza de sangre*

Quevedo, Francisco de, 83, 84

Rauhut, Franz, 33
Recaredo, 67–68, 142n22
recusancy, 40, 46–50, 56
Redondo, Agustín, 6
Regnans in Excelsis, 41, 56
Ricapito, Joseph V., 135Intro nn2–3
Ricart, Domingo, 109
Rico, Francisco, 98, 104
Ricote the Moor, 34, 139n25
Río, Padre Martín del, 137n10
Riley, Edward C., 135n4
Rishton, Edward, 54

163

Index

Rivers, Elias, 6
Rodríguez Luis, Julio, 5–6, 83, 123, 129, 145n25, 149n1, 150n21
Rodríguez Marín, Francisco, 5
Rojas, Fernando de, 1
Rome (Vatican). *See* Pope (Papacy)
Rosales, Luis, 27, 138n15
Rosenkrantz, Dr. Arthur, 144n18
Ruiz de Alarcón, Juan, 147n4
Russell, Peter, 145n27

Saint George, fraternity of, 50
Sáinz de Robles, Federico Carlos, 97
Salamanca, 69, 71, 73, 74, 75, 76, 77, 78, 79, 82, 92
San Bartolomé in Salamanca, college of, 79
Sánchez Ortega, María Teresa, 12, 15, 16, 18, 19, 21, 28, 135ch1 nn1 and 2, 135–36n3, 136nn4 and 6
San Lucar de Barrameda, 50
Santa Hermandad, 20
Santa Teresa, 89
Schiaffino, Rafael, 149n4
Schmiedel, Donald E., 139n2
Selig, Karl-Ludwig, 138n15
Seville, city of, 50, 60, 66, 67
Sicroff, Albert A., 5
Sieber, Harry, 6
Silíceo. *See* Martínez Silíceo, Juan Cardinal
Silverman, Joseph H., 7
Sisebuto, 68
Spanish attitudes toward Italy, 123, 124–25, 125, 128, 130, 131
Spenser, Edmund, 57, 58
Starkie, Walter, 22, 32, 136n7, 138n20
Story, John, 49
Suárez de Figueroa, Cristóbal, 74
Sueños (by Quevedo), 84

Terceira project, 43
ter Horst, Robert, 12, 13
Theogonus, 86
Thompson, Elizabeth Alison, 67, 68
Tiresias, 86
Tirso de Molina, 7
Toledo, Fourth Council of, 68
Tómov, Tomás, 97–98, 104, 147n4
Torre, Guillermo de, 97
Torres Villarroel, Diego de, 79
Treasons Act, 46
Trent, Council of, 82. *See also* Counter-Reformation
Turks, 62–63

U.S.A. Trilogy, 8

Valdés, Alfonso de, 7, 125
Valencia, Pedro de, 143n2
Valencian publishers, 2, 130
Valera, Mosén Diego de, 74
Valladolid, 50, 69, 73
Van Beysterveldt, Antonie A., 98, 99, 100, 108–09, 146n3, 147nn5–8, 148nn10–11
Vatican. *See* Pope (Papacy)
Vega, Lope de, 3, 32, 97–98, 100, 103, 106, 112, 116, 147n4
Velázquez, Jerónimo, 97
Vélez de Guevara, Luis, 84
Verstegan, Richard, 140n8
Vives, Juan Luis, 144n12

Walsingham, Sir Francis, 43
Watkin, Edward I., 41, 48, 49, 54, 55, 59, 140n10
Weiger, John, 5
Wilson, Diana DeArmas, 32

Yare, Sir Miles, 141n12

Zayas, María de, 148n11